LALITAMBA

Number 5

Lalitamba 5
© 2012 Chintamani Books
P.O. Box 131, Planetarium Station
New York, NY 10024
All rights reserved.

Lalitamba ISSN 1930-0662 is published annually in the United States by Chintamani Books. The magazine is printed in accordance with the Sustainable Forestry Initiative.

Cover Art by Pat Lipsky
Dowager (detail)
78 x 61.5 inches
2006-10
oil on linen
© 2012 Pat Lipsky/Artists Rights Society (ARS)

Submission Guidelines: Please submit up to five poems or one work of prose per envelope. Include SASE and contact information (name, address, phone, email). Work should be previously unpublished. Address all correspondence to:

Lalitamba
P.O. Box 131
Planetarium Station
New York, NY 10024

Subscriptions are $12 for one year, plus $4.50 postage and handling.

Lalitamba, Inc. is a 501(c)3 nonprofit organization serving hospitals, prisons, and shelters [www.lalitamba.org]. *Lalitamba* is in partnership with Refuge, a holistic shelter serving the homeless in New York City [www.threejewelsrefuge.org]. Charitable donations are tax-deductible.

The name for the journal was inspired by a devotional song, "Lalitamba, Lalitamba," sung on a pilgrimage through India. In early 2004, we traveled through the country in an effort to alleviate the suffering that comes with poverty, illness, and plain loss of hope. The journal was founded in November of 2004 by Swamini Sri Lalitambika Devi.

The name "Lalitamba" means Divine Mother. In India, the Divine Mother is often thought of as *jagado dharini,* or "she who supports the universe."

TABLE OF CONTENTS

Letters and Prayers . . .

Dear Providence,

In life, we don't get everything we wish for—desire by nature is self-perpetuating, provident, leaves something. . . wanting, which maybe death dispenses. Maybe not. If destiny exists, by definition can we fail to meet it? What choice do we have?

What if we ask: What will I do with my life? Will I marry? Will my marriage end badly? Will it last forever? Happily? Will I have children? Will they like me? Will I like them? Will I comfort them anyway?

What if we don't ask?

When the end comes, will our questions be answered? Or will the answers hail us, as if from receding ice floes? If we stop being, will it dawn on us in advance, a trade-off for the long night after?

If such a night comes, will the universe blanket us at last in sequins of light? Or will it expand to an infinite distance ringed by question marks?

Does all we learn become infinitesimally small next to the growing possibilities of the unknown, the unknowable? Or is knowledge a pregnancy, proceeding to a limit, and then delivering?

Do we ever get past repeating the basics? Was I a good parent? A kind spouse? A helpful neighbor? Was I happy? Were others happy around me?

Did I comfort my children? Teach them to love themselves?

Was I so often in the counting house? In the closet drinking wine? At the neighbor's airing family laundry, pulling weeds in the yard? At the office pulling over-time?

Is anyone happy who doesn't feel blessed? Can we feel blessed without counting our blessings? How do we recognize them? Is it possible to count our blessings with so many of them in disguise, lolling in the shadows between loss and longing? Can happiness be numbered?

Why pursue happiness so relentlessly, if being ends in a heartbeat, a harried pulse done with being counted?

Is having more questions than answers the beginning of understanding?

Corri Elizabeth
Litchfield Park, AZ

dear poet,

at 2:30 in the morning when I wake
wide awake and sleep like color
is eaten by too much black
on the palette and the Milky Way
descends all the way to Earth and Jupiter
is a head lamp in the mine and Scorpio slides
between pines like a dangerous promise—
I am disrupted
I have lost the beat the rhythm
flows on without me and the only way
to catch up is poetry...

I recite your currents of words
over and over I swim them until
they swim me and the Milky Way
becomes our feather boa and we are
cheek to cheek while Jupiter drums and
Scorpio plays the cello

Katherine West
Bellvue, CO

*This journal is
an offering
for liberation.*

Patrice C. Queen

DAUGHTER . . . I AM SORRY

For your many times
Being tortured and in pain
For the locked door
Rights repeatedly denied
Your silenced voice

For the love
You were unable to feel
Instead feeling defiled
Blaming self . . . Asking why
Feeling torn by the four winds

Wondering who to trust
Who to blame
From whence comes help
From where comes pain
You can rise like the Phoenix

I am sorry
I did not hear
The tears falling from your cheeks
Or see the screams
As you cried for help
In your own special way

Janine Canan

THE SAINT

for Amma

The saint sits
under the *bodhi* tree
that I have imagined
in the courtyard of the Hilton

that roars with the machinery
of modern civilization, jet planes
flying low overhead.

She sits in the breeze
that blows through a million dazzling
heart-shaped leaves
amid scents of rose and jasmine.

Closing her eyes, she is like
a statue under the looping limbs
of the ancient tree.

Her brown hands rest
on her foot and on her knee
draped in white silk *sari*.
Silently, she breathes.

And the airplanes are great feathered
birds soaring through the skies.
And the heavens are turning

over a new creation.
And the breezes are soft
with compassion.
And she breathes . . .

Janine Canan

CALL OF RELEASE

To You, I release all
I have received
that is not mine.

Saraswati Ma,
Shakti, Shunya,
Kali Ma, Durga Ma,
Lakshmi and Lalita,

To You I release all
I have swallowed
that is not good.

Oh Wisdom,
Energy, Emptiness,
Destruction, Power,
Abundance and Beauty,

To You I release all
that is not mine,
and never was—
oh Goddesses!

Janine Canan

EVER FLOWING

Narrow stream of the foothills, you are all
that remains of the impetuous Saraswati
that flowed from the Himalayan peaks
across the plains to the sea, on whose banks
a great civilization grew
that worshipped feminine
as well as masculine—
a goddess of a river
that produced a mighty stream of knowledge,
language,
learning,
art,
and grace.
Oh sublime Goddess still revered today—
with your book and lute, water jug and white dress.
Subtle Goddess, we can never forget you,
for we adore you above all others.
For the joy that courses through our daily lives,
thanks. Oh Goddess, oh beauty, to you.

Janine Canan

MIGRATION

Thoughts, thoughts,
thoughts in my shoulders,
thoughts in my knees,
thoughts buried in my toes,
thoughts in my mind,
thoughts, wherever you live,

be gone—like colorful butterflies
fly away—

Janine Canan

WITNESS

Nothing
and everything am I.

Everything
and nothing.

Witness only.
Consciousness.

Ignorance am I
and knowledge.

A baby in her cradle.
A goddess of pure light.

Light am I, and dark.
A star among the multitude.

Janine Canan

WORDS

In every word, there is so much
energy and meaning. A word
does not come from the mind
but from life, grows up

and has its own life history.
A word is historic document.
It's a rich scripture full
of story and wisdom.

A word is a ripening fruit
meant to be plucked at the perfect
moment from the heaving tree.
Pick me, it cries in the strident golden voice
of a woman in her prime, splitting open.

Janine Canan

ABSOLUTE LOVE

Love appallingly holy—
molten, cyclonic, torrential, all-consuming,
unstoppable, unspeakable, unsurpassable,
unbelievable—oh words,

prostrate before this Purity,
dissolve into this Power,
die to this unknowable Truth.

Om Amriteswaryai Namah

Rumi

A BASKET OF FRESH BREAD

The Prophet Muhammed said,
                    "There is no better companion
on this way than what you do. Your actions will be
your best friend, or if you are cruel and selfish,
your actions will be a poisonous snake
that lives in your grave."
                    But tell me,
can you do the good work without a teacher?
Can you even know what is without the presence
of a Master? Notice how the lowest livelihood
requires some instruction.
                    First comes knowledge,
then the doing of the job. And much later,
perhaps after you're dead, something grows
from what you've done.
                    Look for help and guidance
in whatever craft you're learning, look for a generous
teacher, one who has absorbed the tradition he's in.

Look for pearls in oyster shells,
learn technical skill from a craftsman.

Whenever you meet genuine spiritual teachers,
be polite and fair with them.

Ask them questions, and be eager
for answers. Never condescend.
If a master tanner wears an old, threadbare smock,
that doesn't diminish his mastery.

If a fine blacksmith works at the bellows
in a patched apron, it doesn't affect
how he bends the iron.

      Strip away your pride,
and put on humble clothes.

      If you want to learn theory,
talk with theoreticians. That way is oral.

When you learn a craft, practice it.
That learning comes through the hands.

If you want dervishhood, spiritual poverty,
and emptiness you must be friends with a *sheikh*.

Talking about it, reading books, and doing practices
don't help. Soul receives from soul that knowing.
The mystery of spiritual emptiness
may be living in a pilgrim's heart, and yet
the knowing of it may
not yet be his.

Wait for the illuminating openness,
as though your chest was filling with light,
as when God said,

Did we not expand you?

(Qur'an 94:I)

Don't look for it outside yourself.
You are the source of milk. Don't milk others.

There is a milk fountain inside of you.
Don't walk around with an empty bucket.

You have a channel into the ocean, and yet
you ask for water from a little pool.

Beg for that love expansion. Meditate only
on THAT. The Qur'an says,

And He is with you.

(57:4).

There is a basket of fresh bread on your head,
and yet you go from door to door asking for crusts.

Knock on your inner door. No other.
Sloshing knee-deep in fresh riverwater,
you keep wanting a drink from
other people's waterbags.

Water is everywhere around you, but you see only
barriers that keep you from water.

The horse is beneath the rider's thighs, and still
he asks, "Where's my horse?"
                    Right there under you!
"Yes, this is a horse, but where's the horse?"
                    Can't you see!

Yes, I can see, but whoever saw such a horse?"

Mad with thirst, he can't drink from the stream
running so close by his face. He's like a pearl
on the deep bottom, wondering, inside his shell,
Where's the ocean?
                    His mental questionings
form the barrier. His physical eyesight
bandages his knowing. Self- consciousness
plugs his ears.
                    Stay bewildered in God,
                    and only that.

                    Those of you who are scattered,
simplify your worrying lives. There is one
righteousness: Water the fruit trees,
and don't water the thorns. Be generous
to what nurtures the spirit and God's luminous
reason-light. Don't honor what causes
dysentery and knotted up-tumors.
Don't feed both sides of yourself equally.
The spirit and the body carry different loads
and require different attentions.

Too often
we put saddlebags on Jesus and let the donkey
run loose in the pasture.

Don't make the body do
what the spirit does best, and don't put a big load
on the spirit that the body could carry easily.

Translated by Coleman Barks
Reprinted with permission from
The Essential Rumi
(Harper Collins, 2004), p. 254.

Coleman Barks

A COMMENTARY POEM . . .

There is a passage in Book V
of Rumi's *Masnavi*, 11. 1073 ff.
Someone with a basket on his head of fragrant,
just-baked bread goes door to door
begging for a crust. This is how
we appear to Rumi, knee-deep in a freshwater creek,
asking for someone's waterbag. The cure for thirst is
more close by than that.
A man riding a horse wonders,
Where's my horse? Under you. You are riding it.
Yes, but what kind of horse is this?
A pearl in deep ocean
wonders inside its shell, Where *is* the ocean?
Stay bewildered in the present, fully awake.
Feel this horse you ride as water feels an aqueduct.
A beautiful scent surrounds you
of the answer you carry
in a basket balanced (unconsciously?) on your head.
Breath, pulse-throb, eyesight, the big artery
on your neck,
ears that usher music in. You are a cooking egg
in the skillet ordering *one over medium*. You are
the waterwheel in a hard rain river hoping to turn.
Well sure, I feel this motion, but I want to *turn*.

Vivekanand Jha

AN INTERVIEW WITH JAYANTA MAHAPATRA

Jayanta Mahapatra needs little introduction. He is often considered to be the most prolific poet in the history of Indian English poetry. A voice apart from the Bombay school of poets, he is known to have shared a special bond with poet A. K. Ramanujan, and offers a profundity of unique images, symbols, and themes.

Jayanta Mahapatra is a scholar of scientific background. Throughout his life, he has taught physics at various universities throughout Orissa. Meanwhile, he is the first poet to receive the Sahitya Akademi Award for Indian English Poetry. He has written 16 books of poetry, including *Relationship*, *Bare Face*, *Shadow Space*, and *Door of Paper: Essays and Memoirs*.

It was a morning in November of 2009 that I had the opportunity to visit the residence of Jayanta Mahapatra. Jayanta Mahapatra is in his nineties. He has been a patient of chronic asthma and recurrent migraine headaches. Because of chest heaviness and breathlessness, he prefers not to talk in the morning. I returned empty handed that morning, but later in the evening I was able to talk with him.

After the passing of his wife, the late Runu Mahapatra, Jayanta Mahapatra is internally shaken, weakened. They were an ideal couple.

After meeting with him, I came out of his room and spoke to his maidservant about how Jayanta Mahapatra feels in the absence of his wife. Having served them for years, she said that Jayanta Mahapatra wept bitterly when his wife died and that, even now, he occasionally bursts into tears in her loving memory.

Let us share the excerpts of conversation.

Jha: I would like to know about your reaction to talk of your being the father of modern and postmodern Indian English poetry.

Mahapatra: No, no. I write what I can. I don't think about that.

Jha: Can you recall the moment that inspired you to compose maiden verse?

Mahapatra: Actually, I was writing stories in the beginning, but these stories were not published. They were all rejected. So, I didn't write all day long. I did research in physics. In photography, I also had an interest. Then, later on, I began writing. I don't know how it happened. Very late, it happened.

Jha: To whom would you dedicate your success as a poet.

Mahapatra: It's my wife. She has been very cooperative. She has been giving me freedom. If your wife doesn't give you freedom, how can you write? Somebody should be there. You take the time also and also worries, but no worries from other things, household things and all like that. So, if you have time, and then she gives you freedom also to live, you want to live to help people.

Jha: Is your madame surviving or not?

Mahapatra: No, she is no more.

Jha: Is *Chandrabhaga* (a biannual literary journal) still publishing or not?

Mahapatra: We are not publishing it now. I didn't have time. I didn't have the money involved for publishing. All these sorts of problems take over. That's why we stopped it.

Jha: In a country of more than one billion people, the magazine *Chandrabhaga* has come to cease publication. In your view what is the fate and future of Indian English poetry?

Mahapatra: Graphic magazines, fashion magazines, movie magazines, you can only get funding for these. Otherwise, nobody is purchasing a literary periodical. Not only in India. I think this is the case everywhere in the world, but especially in India. We have too much emphasis on film and fashion.

Jha: I have read your various interviews, articles, and essays, and found that you were never mentioned with the great names like Shakespeare, Wordsworth, Keats, T.S. Eliot, and W. B. Yeats. Does this make you someone unconventional?

Mahapatra: I don't know. I didn't study them. I studied science, you know. English literature, I didn't read.

Jha: Sir you express your dissatisfaction over the absence of constructive criticism on your poetry, especially in India. They include only ugly aspects of your poetry. What kind of criticism do you want to have on your poetry?

Mahapatra: I don't read criticism. I haven't seen those books. I don't want to see criticism, because that doesn't help me much—unless it is positive criticism. But one writes for what one writes. One doesn't write because the critic tells one to write like this.

Jha: What is your main source of inspiration?

Mahapatra: Main source of inspiration? My land, my people, my place, what I see, what social injustice I see, and political injustice. I should like to write about hunger. I think Orissa is the one of the very, very, very, very poor states. Very poor. You go inside the villages. You will see they don't have a place to live in. They don't have a roof over their heads. They don't have one meal a day. They don't even have rice to eat. During election times, politicians visit the villages once, and then for the next five years nothing happens. The same poverty continues. The people sell their children to keep their own stomachs full. Mothers sell their daughters. Fathers sell their daughters. Even today it's happening, especially in Orissa and the interior of India.

Jha: In your autobiography you have talked about a beautiful girl.

Mahapatra: Irene! Irene! I have talked about other girls also. But this autobiography is in the language Oriya. In English you can't do that. In your own mother tongue you can talk about those things that you can't talk about in English. What we have by virtue of our soil and local air that we can't have any other way, we have with our mother tongue.

I have one and only one religion—that if I couldn't help anybody why should I harm. (*Apani mitti se, apani hawa se jo hoti hai wo bahar ke raste se nahin. Apani maa ke juwan se hoti hai. Mera to ek hin dharma hai ki kisi ka kuchh harm mat karo. Ham to kisi ke liye kuchh kar nahin pate hai to kisi ko dukh kyon pahuchayen.*). If we can't help somebody, let us not harm somebody. That should be the religion of everybody. Religion has no concern with temple, church, or mosque.

Jha: I came to know from your autobiography that you have received your M.Sc. from Patna.

Mahapatra: That's right, from Patna, Patna Science College.

Jha: As I am from Bihar, I would like to know about your experience there during the course of post-graduate study at Patna University.

Mahapatra: Those days were much better than today. Patna University was one of the best universities of India. I was living in a small mess with a small verandah—a small rented building. We were about ten students. We rented rooms from a professor of the engineering college, Professor Ojha. The building in which we were staying was near to the Mahendru Ghat and the law college.

Jha: Your autobiography describes your life up until 1989. Are you planning to write or have written about yourself after that?

Mahapatra: I have written a small portion of my autobiography in English, because an American encyclopedia wanted it for a section on living contemporary writers, but now I am writing the autobiography in Oriya. It's being serialized in a magazine.

Jha: Does it tell of your life after 1989.

Mahapatra: No, no, no, it's about my childhood and early days.

Jha: Has it been published?

Mahapatra: I am just writing it now. It will come out soon, part by part, in a series. I am trying to write. I don't know if I will pull on. I can't tell of tomorrow. (*Kal ki baat to ham nahin bol sakate.*). But I am trying to do whatever I can. It's all about my childhood, my youth, and my days at Patna.

Jha: The theme of your poetry, too, is oriented towards childhood.

Mahapatra: Yah, all my childhood.

Jha: You have talked about some emerging poets from the North-East region.

Mahapatra: There are some good young poets, especially from Meghalay, Mizoram, and also in Arunachal Pradesh.

Jha: Earlier, such talents were not there in that region. How now do we happen to see such things?

Mahapatra: See, tension is there in the North-East. If you have no tension, you can't write well. If you have tension, you can bring about your feelings well. Unless you have failure, suffering, and sorrows in your life, how can you write? If you have enough to eat, enough money, a good house, and a car, why will you write? What will you write about? You have no problems to write about.

If you have got problems—these may be racial problems, religious problems, hunger problems, and social problems—the problems will lead you to think. Unless you think, you can't write. Ideas will not come into your mind. For ideas, you need the images to supplement your ideas. So, all things make a certain cycle that is necessary. It begins only when you have certain problems in your life, starting to write poetry. Isn't it right?

Jha: You have talked about one poet from Kolkata.

Mahapatra: You talk about Rudhra Kinshuk. I like this poet. He's a young boy, and he makes good use of new images. I like when you put a new type of image in the poem.

Jha: What do you mean by "new images"? Innovation, it should be extracted from the new invention—science and technology.

Mahapatra: "New images" means you try to bring about something that never happened or has not been done by other poets before you. There was a great Urdu poet from Allahabad, Faiz Ahmad Faiz. He used to write, "I want to drink through eyes not by lips." (*Lavon se nahin. Main peena chahata, main ankhoon se peena chahata hoon.*) Something new like this.

Jha: Now, writing is your main sort of engagement.

Mahapatra: I read also a lot. When I can't read, I write. When I can't write, I read.

Jha: The very titles of your books, *A Rain of Rites*, *Shadow Space*, *Bare Face*, *Lies of Dawn*, bear signs of bleakness and barrenness. Is there a vested interest in doing that?

Mahapatra: No, it came on its own, on its own.

Jha: What are the works you are at present busy with?

Mahapatra: At present, I am writing my autobiography in Oriya. At least one part I want to publish by June, if I am living. (*Mahapatra smiles.*) After I finish it, I will publish a new book of English poems. So let me see what happens.

Jha: In the book, *History of Indian English Literature*, authored by M. K. Naik, he mentions that many contemporary Indian poets who made a name in Indian English poetry were first published by P. Lal. Is it true?

Mahapatra: It is true that many people were published by P. Lal. He has done a very good job, a very good humanitarian job. We can't deny it. Giving encouragement to new writers is something not many people have done. The poet, Ezekiel, even this man who made a name, Vikram Seth, he was also published by P. Lal. Kamala Das. All these people.

Jha: What would be your advice to the budding poet?

Mahapatra: Write whatever you feel, feel from your heart, from your inside. One thing also will help you. You just write from the level and tilt to a little higher level. If you can, go towards God in the guise of writing. (*Thora eshawar ke taraph, thora sa, aagar hamlog ja sakate hain likhake.*)

    If we can, that should be our goal. Don't you think so?

    Your conscience and soul search out good things. So, when you go about writing, write a poem as a priest makes offerings to God, by picking and choosing the flowers; so we should do with words. (*Jaise Poojari phool chun-chun kar chadhate hain to hamlog. Pooja ke tarahshabad ko aik-aik kar ke banana chahiye. Mera to yahin khyal hai.*)

Jayanta Mahapatra

FREEDOM

At times, as I watch,
it seems as though my country's body
floats down somewhere on the river.
Left alone, I grow into
half-disembodied bamboo,
its lower part sunk
into itself on the bank.

Here, old widows and dying men
cherish their freedom,
bowing time after time in obstinate prayers,
while children scream
with this desire for freedom
to transform the world
without even laying hands on it.

In my blindness, at times I fear
I'd wander back to either of them.
In order for me not to lose face,
it is necessary for me to be alone,
not to meet the woman and her child
in that remote village in the hills
who never had even a little rice
for their one daily meal, these fifty years,
and not to see the uncaught, bloodied light
of sunsets cling to tall white columns of Parliament House.

In the new temple man has built nearby,
the priest is the one who knows freedom,
while God hides in the dark like an alien.
Each day that I keep looking for the light,
shadows find excuses to keep.
Trying to find the only freedom I know,
the freedom of the body when it's alone,
the freedom of the silent shale, the moonless coal,
the beds of streams of the sleeping God,
I keep the ashes away,
try not to wear them on my forehead.

Jayanta Mahapatra

ASH

The substance that stirs in my palm
could well be a dead man; no need
to show surprise at the dizzy acts of wind.
My old father sitting uncertainly three feet away

is the slow cloud against the sky:
so my heart's beating makes of me a survivor
over here where the sun quietly sets.
The ways of freeing myself:

the glittering flowers, the immensity of rain, for example,
which were limited to promises once,
have had to lie to themselves. And the wind,
that had made simple revelation in the leaves,

plays upon the ascetic-faced vision of waters;
and without thinking
something makes me keep close to the walls
as though I were afraid of that justice in the shadows.

Now the world passes into my eye:
the birds flutter toward rest around the tree,
the clock jerks each memory towards
the present to become a past, floating away
like ash, over the bank.

My own stirrings like the wind's
keep hoping for the solace that would be mine
in my father's eyes,
to pour the good years back to me;

the dead man who licks my palms
is more likely to encourage dark intolerance
rather than turn me
toward some strangely solemn charade:

the dumb order of the myth
lined up in the life-field,
the unconcerned wind perhaps truer than the rest,
rustles the empty, bodiless grains.

Vivekanand Jha

THE INDIAN GIRL

Hey Indian girl!
With you I have something to share,
If you would like to hear me.
You used to put on priceless ornaments
Moulded not by goldsmith
But in God's firmament.

There was shyness in your eyes.
I look for it often,
But I think now she dies.

You never used to forget
Your bosoms to cover
For which the Indian woman
Is known the world over.

The house used to be a temple
In which you would reside.
It now looks abandoned
As in bar and club you preside.

On account of your religion
The world was at peace.
You're being materialistic
Dispossessed of all bliss.

On your ancient garments
India used to pride.
On your new attire
We find no places
For our faces to hide.

You were identified
One in a million
By virtue of your pendants,
bangles and vermilion.

You are now nowhere
In the list of beauty
As you have joined
The club of nudity.

Though you claim to
be virgin and chaste
I think you have made
Your decisions in haste.

It is as good as
Attaining divinity
To find the fiancee
Of authentic virginity.

Vivekanand Jha

ODE TO FAME

All causes of evils, oh Fame.
To achieve you one crosses
All limits of shame.

One makes an excuse lame.
One encashes another's name.
Upon others one transfers
One's own blame.

Achievements of others someone claims.
One sets houses of others aflame.
One plays a back-biting game.
One abducts the mother's gem.
One dispossesses another's dame.

One explores a deadly den.
A country suffers brain drain.
One has to descend from heaven to lane.
Others have to suffer for personal gain.
One puts one's reputation on the wane.
With your increasing offspring, oh fame,
It isn't possible for scandal and scam to tame.

Jyotsna Sreenivasan

SISTER

My sister has decided to come to the family reunion, after all. Medhya is scheduled to arrive at our parents' house tonight, Thursday evening, a day before the other guests.

That was my idea—that she come early and hang out with us—but now I'm starting to regret insisting that she show up at all.

Medhya didn't want anyone to pick her up from the Cleveland airport, so Dad and I are sitting here in the family room, pretending to mind our own business. He's watching the news on TV, and I'm flipping through an issue of *India Abroad*, not reading any of it. Mom's in the kitchen, lifting the lids of the pans. We're waiting for Medhya to arrive. Then Mom will start frying the *dosas*. *Masala dosa* is Medhya's favorite meal. My husband, Sandeep, has to work late tonight, and so isn't able to join us for dinner. I think he's glad to stay away.

The table is set, and everything is ready for dinner. Mom is dressed well, as usual—a new tan linen pantsuit. She's even made up her face with lipstick and eyeliner. She looks considerably younger than her fifty years. She walks four miles a day and is very strict with herself about fried foods and sweets.

"Don't get your hopes up, Sudha," Dad shouts to Mom from the family room. He doesn't bother to turn towards my mother, but directs his shout at the television screen. Dad isn't even fully dressed. He's wearing an undershirt and a stained pair of sweatpants.

Mom crashes her lids louder. "It is my birthday," she yells. "What is wrong with my daughter coming home for my birthday?"

"We are talking about Medhya," Dad shouts. "She will never change."

Over the years, I've learned to ignore my parents' sniping, but this evening it makes me even more nervous than I already am. I throw aside the newspaper, rush into the kitchen, and grab my purse off the counter.

"Where are you going?" Mom demands. She's using a paper towel to rub away a spot of *dosa* batter on her blouse.

"My list," I mumble.

I pull out a tattered sheet of paper from my purse and look at it, yet again. Tomorrow, I'll buy the fruits for the Saturday picnic. We still have to get ice. The charcoal is in the garage of our house—I have to remind Sandeep to bring it over. I'll go to Szalay's and pick out the freshest ears of corn. I also need to call the restaurant to re-confirm our reservation for Sunday.

I started thinking about what we could do for Mom's fiftieth birthday a year ago—on her forty-ninth. I wanted Mom to feel really special. Mom loves parties and celebrations. In fact, she has the reputation for being one of the most capable entertainers in our Indian community. When Medhya and I were teenagers, she'd pay us $2 per hour to act as "the maids" at dinners she gave for our friends. We passed around the pop and appetizers, set up the dinner buffet on the dining table, and took our stations at the sink and dishwasher after dinner was over. Of course, she never told anyone she was paying us, so everyone was impressed that Mom had such helpful, well-behaved daughters. Even now, at least two or three times a year, she cooks a full Indian meal (including two appetizers and dessert) for thirty couples all by herself. She enjoys the adulation as everyone gushes, "How do you do it, Sudha?"

I've always wanted to plan a family reunion like this, so that my mother could enjoy herself and not have to do any work. We have relatives coming in from all over the U.S. and Canada.

I guess, if there is any ulterior motive for this party, it's to get Medhya together with my parents again. My sister hasn't spoken to Mom and Dad for six years, since Sandeep and I got married. The thing I've most wanted, all my life, is a happy family. In elementary school, I remember reading the *Little House* books and longing for a family as close as the Ingalls family. In junior high, I remember watching "The Cosby Show" and wanting the Huxtables to be my family. It sounds silly now. I know life isn't like a book or a TV show. But that's what I've always wanted—a family where people could talk to each other without shouting, listen without making snide remarks, and support each other. All the stuff we never had as children.

I didn't have any big plan to get Medhya to make up with Mom and Dad, but I was hoping I could convince her to help me plan the reunion. I thought that, if she had a hand in planning it, she might feel more ownership of the whole thing, and who knew what might happen? Also, she could stand to do something to help others, instead of just wallowing in her own misery. But whenever I brought up the subject of the reunion, she told me she might not even show up for it. I knew, and I'm sure she knew too, that this would hurt our mother a lot. Even if Medhya doesn't want to admit it, Mom loves both of her daughters. She really does want Medhya to be happy.

It took me a long time to convince Mom that we should even have this reunion. Whenever I tried to talk to her about her birthday, she'd say, "No one has big parties for the fiftieth birthday. I will let you do something special for my sixtieth."

The sixtieth birthday is an important milestone in India. In the past I guess a lot of people didn't live that long. Now, of course, just about all my relatives are able to celebrate their sixtieth birthdays, but we still make a fuss over the whole thing.

"Why wait ten years?" I'd say. "Your birthday's in August, Mom. That's the perfect time for a reunion. Wouldn't it be great to get everyone together? We haven't all been together in so long. Probably not since Sandeep and I got married."

"People will think it is crazy for me to have a big birthday, just because I turned fifty," Mom would say. And, "I don't want to be doing all that cooking for my own birthday."

Then she'd sigh, like she was tired from just thinking about it. She always likes to pretend she can't handle doing too much, and then she pulls out all the stops at the last minute and impresses everyone.

"Where will they all stay? I can't have them all here. I don't have enough towels and sheets. We can't ask them to stay at a hotel. How will I manage? Your father is not so young, to be driving to the airport and picking so many people up."

She had a whole bag full of concerns such as these.

I went through them one by one: I would do the cooking. We'd have the actual birthday luncheon at a restaurant. I was sure some people wouldn't mind staying in a hotel for such a special occasion. Sandeep would be happy to help pick up guests.

But still, she resisted. I kept after her, because I knew she'd enjoy getting together with everyone.

Then suddenly, about four months ago, she called me up and said I should go ahead and plan the reunion.

"You mean it?" I asked.

"It's so nice that you want to do this for your mother. You are so busy as it is."

"I'm not that busy, Mom. I don't even have kids yet." Sandeep and I have been trying to get pregnant ever since we got married.

I called Medhya and told her the reunion was on, and that's when she started saying she didn't think she'd come. "Everyone will look at me and say, oh, there's Medhya the failure."

I've never heard any of our relatives refer to Medhya as a "failure," but I'm sure they've thought it, since I've thought it myself plenty of times.

I tried to reassure her. "Medhya, they'll just be happy to see you. A lot of them haven't seen you since our wedding."

"Yeah." Deep sigh. "I don't know if I'll be happy to see them, though. Everyone will have some impressive news about themselves, and I'll have nothing."

I could relate to that. I know I shouldn't be jealous, but sometimes I just don't want to hear, one more time, about my cousin Arvind's fabulous medical research fellowship, my cousin Saumya's new five-bedroom house, and how my cousin Deepa can take care of three children under five with absolutely no household help. Mom keeps up with all her nieces and nephews, and is sure to tell me their various conquests.

"Oh, come on, Medhya. It won't be so bad. I'm counting on you to help me."

"Vineeta, this is your idea. Mom will probably be upset if it doesn't turn out exactly the way she wants."

I was afraid of that too. But all I said was, "Aren't you going to help out at all?"

Medhya didn't say anything, and as it turned out, she didn't help at all.

Why was I surprised?

At least Medhya decided to show up, though I'm a little worried about why she decided to show up. Is she planning some sort of confrontation with Mom and Dad? Is she going to ruin this whole thing on purpose?

* * *

The doorbell rings. I stuff my list back into my purse and rush to open the door. "Medhya!" I exclaim. I'm shocked at her appearance but try to keep a smile on my face. She's wearing a faded pair of jeans and dirty white sneakers. On her back is a large camping-style backpack. She's thinner than I ever remember seeing her.

She steps in and gives me a tight hug. "Hi, you." Her eyes stray past me for a second, and then she glances at the floor. I turn around and see Mom standing in the kitchen doorway with a bright smile on her face.

"Medhya! Come give your mother a hug." Mom's voice is high and extra-cheerful.

Medhya says nothing to Mom, but mumbles to me, "Let me put this stuff upstairs."

I turn to give Mom a sympathetic glance, but she has disappeared from the doorway. I follow Medhya upstairs and show her the room. This is not the house we grew up in. My parents moved to a larger, fancier one in a brand-new subdivision, after both of us left home. Most of my parents' friends "traded up" after their kids finished college.

Even though this is not the house we grew up in, Mom has reserved two rooms as "Vineeta's" and "Medhya's." The rooms look nothing like our childhood bedrooms. Mom has furnished each with new queen-sized beds, matching dressers and chests, and has decorated the walls with *batiks* and embroidered tapestries.

Medhya drops her backpack with a thud.

"I'm staying in this room with you during the reunion." I point to my suitcase near the closet. "Radha Auntie will be using the other bedroom, and Sandeep will be driving in from home." To tell the truth, I hadn't really wanted to stay in the same room with Medhya, but I didn't want to inflict her on anyone else.

"That's good." She gives me a smile. Then, she sits on the floor and starts unzipping her backpack.

"Let's go downstairs. Mom's making *masala dosa*."

"No thanks." She removes an embroidered pouch from her backpack.

"What do you mean, no thanks? It's your favorite."

"Not anymore," she says. "I only eat raw food. Do you realize that cooking actually prevents food from being normally metabolized by the human body?"

"You mean you're not going to eat dinner with us?"

"I've got some snacks in my backpack."

I go downstairs and tell Mom that Medhya won't be eating dinner. Mom doesn't say a word but immediately turns on the stove, oils the pan, and begins spreading the *dosa* batter in thin, efficient spirals. I stand by the stove and feel useless.

"Go sit down!" Mom scolds. She's stressed out and so is taking it out on me. I do as I'm told. I'm used to obeying my parents.

Mom slaps a plate with one *dosa* in front of me.

"What did I tell you?" Dad calls from the family room.

"She is tired from her trip," Mom shouts back.

"You watch. She will not say one word to you until she leaves."

Mom rushes back to the stove. "I am not going to serve you in there."

Dad leaves the TV on and shuffles to his favorite spot at the table, from which he can still see the screen. Mom slaps another plate in front of him.

I feel sick to my stomach. How can Dad be so cruel? How can Medhya be so cruel? This is really Medhya's fault. What parents wouldn't be stressed out by a daughter who refuses to speak to them?

After Mom and Dad go up to bed at 11 o'clock, I call Sandeep and tell him briefly how everything's going.

His only comment: "Don't let her bother you."

Easy for him to say. He doesn't have a crazy sister to deal with.

I'm about to head upstairs myself when I hear Medhya creeping down. She sinks into the recliner in the family room and pulls one of Mom's hand-crocheted afghans over her. I sit on the sofa across from her.

"How's your job?" I ask lightly. It's the only non-controversial thing I can think of to ask. I'm angry that she's started out this weekend by shunning our parents, but I don't dare say anything to set her off.

"I don't have one."

"What?"

"I was fired."

Oh, great. She very conveniently lost her job just before the reunion, so she'd have a giant sob story to lay on us. I don't really want to hear about her job. Whatever the problem is, I'm sure she won't let me help her. But I guess I should be supportive.

"What happened?" I ask.

"Bill hates women," she says, looking at the floor.

Bill is her boss. "He hates women?"

"Yeah. He's a male chauvinist. I should probably sue him." She's huddled under the afghan, even though it's August.

"Are you cold?" I ask. "Should I turn down the air-conditioning?"

She shrugs but doesn't say anything. She just keeps staring at the floor.

I want to leap across the room, grab her by the shoulders, and shake her like a rag doll. What is the matter with her? Why does she turn into this pitiful wreck every time she enters my presence?

She's not like this with other people. She actually has a lot of friends, and I know she's not this puddle of wretchedness with them.

She's had lots of boyfriends, too. Not that it's led to anything stable. The guys she picks are always the inappropriate, co-dependent, mutually destructive kind. I can never understand it—she's a lot prettier than I am and lots of decent guys drool over her.

I know I should be more patient with Medhya. I have this feeling that she's actually not well—I mean, that there might be some kind of mental imbalance there. Nothing unusual, but maybe depression or something like that. In the past, whenever I suggested that she see a counselor or a doctor about her problems she'd say, "Anyone who survived our family is bound to have something wrong with them. Our whole family is so dysfunctional." But as far as I know, she's never taken the initiative to see any kind of professional.

I wonder if she thinks I'm dysfunctional too. I've never asked, and I don't want to know. Sometimes, I wish Medhya weren't my sister.

Maybe she wishes the same thing. Maybe if I weren't around, being the obedient daughter, her behavior wouldn't seem so bad.

Medhya's not the kind of sister I want. I want a sister I can pal around with. I want a sister who gets married and has babies, so we can share maternity clothes and baby clothes and parenting stories. I want a sister who has a steady enough income that we can plan trips to Paris, or the Virgin Islands, or someplace, just the two of us. I want a sister who's normal.

But Medhya's all I've got, and now that she's here for the reunion, I really want to be patient with her. I want things to go well in her life. I want things to go well this weekend. I don't want to make her even more upset. I take a deep breath and tell myself that the best thing I can do is just listen to what she has to say.

"What exactly did Bill do?" I ask.

"Oh." She looks at me like she expected me to have forgotten the subject. "Just everything. He pays the men more than he pays the women. He gives the men better assignments. He promotes them faster. I've been keeping track. This one guy who was hired months after me got assigned one of our biggest clients. That client should have gone to me."

"Maybe there's some other reason?"

"Like what? Like I don't have a college degree—is that what you mean? Bill knew I didn't have the degree, when he hired me. He said it didn't matter. If it didn't matter then, it shouldn't matter now. I'm doing good work. I deserve at least equal treatment."

"But you said you were fired. How did that happen?"

She's silent for a moment. Then she says, "I sent around this protest petition at the office. I asked all the women to sign it. Bill found out about it, and he fired me. He fired me for standing up for my own rights, Vineeta." She gives me a wounded look.

I only half-believe Medhya's story. I'm sure her boss is a pig, but Medhya has always been determined to do herself in. Why the need for a public petition? Why does she have to be so flamboyant about everything?

Like the lack of a college degree. That's another example of how she's destroyed herself in order to rebel against our parents. At least that's how I see it. She practically failed high school, and then she spent three years at Kent State without working towards any kind of degree. She took classes in horticulture, tap dancing, pottery, beekeeping, jazz piano, and sign language. It seemed like she was choosing classes randomly, by flipping a coin. I could never figure out what she was up to. I know she's really smart. She's always been better than me at a lot of things, like adding up numbers in her head and remembering the capitals of all the countries in the world. (Dad used to drill us on those kind of things when we were in grade school.)

But the last couple of years of high school, her grades slipped. Her teachers would tell Mom and Dad that Medhya was smart but that she wasn't "applying herself."

Mom and Dad would scold her and tell her that she had to work harder. Dad said he wouldn't pay for her college, if she didn't improve her grades, and she said she didn't care. Mom told her that no Indian boy would agree to marry her, if she didn't have a college degree, and she said she hated Indians.

"I've realized something important," Medhya says. "The fact that I don't have a college degree is connected to what my boss is doing. Our entire society is designed to keep women down and out. Why did Mom and Dad want me to go to college? So they could find me a rich husband, right? It had absolutely nothing to do with my own development or self-worth. Now, my boss is doing the exact same thing. We just can't win, Vineeta."

Why is she putting me in the same boat? I have "won," in a sense. I have the college degree. Who cares why Mom and Dad wanted me to get one? I didn't have to destroy my life to prove anything to them. I mean, sometimes parents actually do have good ideas.

In college I had trouble deciding what I wanted to major in. Really, if it hadn't been for my parents, I might have just skipped college and become a hairdresser. That's what I enjoyed doing at that age. I learned how to cut hair from a friend in high school, and I used to give $5 haircuts to other girls in my classes. I never even brought up that idea with my parents, for obvious reasons.

During my first year of college, I was leaning towards a degree in elementary education. Dad said I wouldn't make enough money, and Mom said teachers are not respected. I ended up majoring in accounting, which is what Mom wanted me to do. I guess I didn't care enough about it to fight, especially not to fight about it just for the sake of fighting, the way Medhya seems to. That's the one thing I hate more than anything—fighting and conflict. Sandeep jokes that I'd rather disappear than fight.

Anyway, accounting was fine. I ended up liking it after all, and I do make good money now. It turned out to be the right decision.

I didn't see anything wrong with letting my parents introduce me to potential husbands, either. Sandeep was one of the grad students from South India that Mom was always adopting and inviting home for dinner. When Mom and Dad asked if I would consider marrying him, I agreed to meet with him. Since it wasn't just a first date but a meeting about marriage, we talked about all sorts of important things, like how we felt about debt, how many children we wanted, and whether I'd mind having his parents stay with us for a few months when they visited from India.

I thought we could get along. I wasn't in love with him when we got married, but since when is being in love a good predictor of success in marriage? I figured if we were both committed to the marriage, it would work out fine, and it has. I was just looking for a guy who's easy to talk to—someone with whom I wouldn't feel lonely, the way I felt so often growing up.

I look at Medhya. She is huddled under the afghan. I want to say something helpful. She'll probably take it the wrong way. "Medhya, I don't know why you took that job anyway. You told me you didn't even like marketing. Maybe this is for the best."

"I have no savings, Vineeta. It's not for the best. I took the job because I needed more money. They said I'd get on-the-job training and the salary was a lot better than what I was making at Rigby's. I'm a single woman, remember, Vineeta? I can't depend on a husband to support me. I have to look out for myself."

Is this comment directed at me? I certainly don't depend on my husband to support me—I am gainfully employed, after all. It's true that Sandeep does make more money than I do, and our plan is that I'll stay home while our children are young, but I haven't told Medhya this. She doesn't even know we're trying to get pregnant.

Anyway, whose fault is it that Medhya remains single? She certainly hasn't done a very good job of "looking out for herself." All of her jobs have been boring or frustrating or both, to hear her tell it. Her jobs have also, coincidentally, driven my parents crazy.

She moved to Newark, New Jersey for this latest job. And why Newark? She could have moved anywhere. She's single and free.

Before that, she was a bartender at this sports bar called Rigby's in Cleveland. Before that, a shuttle driver for a hotel. Before that, a waitress. In college she worked as a nude art model, which she actually told my parents about. She could have kept it a secret. It was just a little part-time job. She, however, felt compelled to reveal all, so to speak. Dad practically had a heart attack, but what could he do? She was living on her own, in a filthy, falling-apart old house she shared with a bunch of other students, all of whom just happened to be men.

Maybe I shouldn't ask this, but I can't help myself. Who does she think she is, barging in to throw her wet blanket of anger and resentment on this celebration? "Medhya, why are you still so angry at Mom and Dad?

Her head rears up off the back of the recliner. I can see the tendons standing out on her neck. "Do you realize," she hisses, "that I got straight A's every year until tenth grade, and Dad never said one word to me about it? Then, in tenth grade, I got a B in social studies. I didn't even realize I wasn't doing well. We had that crazy Mr. Matting for a teacher. He'd mostly make us work in small groups, and then he'd leave the room. Anyway, I got a B the first grading period. All Dad said was, 'Medhya, I'm disappointed. You can do better than this.' I was so hurt. He never said anything about all the A's I got. Nothing was ever good enough for him. I got an A in social studies the next grading period, and what did Dad say? Nothing. I saw him pick up my report card, look at it, and toss it aside."

Medhya is breathless. I wish she'd stop. I remember what it was like. It wasn't so different for me, either. Some years ago, I was helping my parents move from our old house to this one. I was sorting through a bunch of junk in the dresser of my old bedroom. I found a box with school stuff in it—my grades and clippings from the high school newspaper. I sat right there on the bare mattress and started reading through all of it. I was surprised at what I read, that I hadn't been a bad student at all.

My memory of the school years was that I had been an "average" student. This is what my parents called me, and it was no compliment. Among our Indian friends, anyone with "average" grades was basically considered stupid.

But the things I was reading told a different story. My grades had been mostly A's and some B's. In fact, that whole box of stuff made me smile, including a photo of me standing with the other National Merit Scholar semi-finalists. I don't remember being in that photo. I only remember my father's disgust. Well, not really disgust—more like an "I-never-thought-you'd-make-it-anyway" attitude. This, when I did not actually become a National Merit Scholar.

I put the box of stuff in my car and took it home with me. I was still smiling, when I told Sandeep about it. Only later, lying in bed in the darkness of our bedroom, did I stop smiling. How could my parents have lied to me? They'd made me believe I was stupid, when I was nothing of the sort.

I couldn't sleep. I got up and used the toilet. I lay down again. I felt itchy all over.

I got up again, went downstairs, and drank a glass of water. Then, I went back upstairs. I was exhausted.

Sandeep rolled over and sighed. "What's wrong?"

"Nothing." I never like sharing negative feelings. I'm always afraid they'll spill over and get out of control.

"Come on. Tell me." He put his arm around me. "It's not good to keep things inside."

So, I told him.

"Of course you're not stupid," he murmured. "No one thinks you're stupid. When your father first talked to me about marrying you, all he could talk about was how smart you are."

"Why didn't he ever tell me that? Why did they lie to me? Why did they try to make me think I was stupid?" I dug my fingernails into my palm to keep from crying. If I started crying, I knew it would be a flood.

"You know how Indian parents are," Sandeep said.

"No, I actually don't know how Indian parents are. I wasn't raised in India, remember?"

"OK, don't get so upset. It's just that they think if they praise too much, the child will become complacent and lazy. That's all. Your dad wanted you to work hard."

I waited, until I heard Sandeep's even breathing. When I was sure he was asleep, I slid out from under the covers and went downstairs. I couldn't stand it when Sandeep defended my parents, when he pretended to understand them better than I did.

I sat in the dining room in the dark. I sat for a long time, maybe an hour. Finally, I thought of something. Maybe my parents were right. Maybe, if I had worked harder, I could have done better. Maybe Mom and Dad hadn't been lying to me.

I went back upstairs and crawled into bed. I willed myself to lie still, and after a long time, I fell asleep.

So you see, whatever pain Mom and Dad caused me, I got over it. I know they only wanted the best for me. I didn't let it keep me from living my life.

Why can't Medhya get over it?

"Mom was happy with your grades," I point out, trying to pacify her.

"Sure." She rolls her eyes. "Yeah, Mom was happy, so she could brag to all her Indian friends about what a smart daughter she had."

"What's wrong with that? She was proud of you."

"All she cared about was putting on a good face for the rest of the Indian community. Remember that time she found the suicide note?"

I remember, although I don't want to.

The only reason Mom found the note was that Medhya had left it on the kitchen counter, right by the answering machine. As if Mom could miss it. The memory makes my gut twist. From frustration? From despair? My sister was only 16. She was just a kid. Mom should have handled it better.

As soon as Mom found the note, she called me down from my room, where I was studying. I was 18 at the time. I had just started my first year of college.

"Do you know anything about this?" she'd asked, and thrust the note into my hand. She seemed angry. The note was fairly short. It said, *I wish I were dead. I want to kill myself. I deserve a knife in my heart.* I remember the note. It has haunted me for years, even though I only read it once. I didn't want to know that my little sister had thoughts like these.

"What does this mean?" Mom had asked. She seemed so angry that I thought she assumed I wrote the note.

"It's Medhya's," I remember saying. I didn't understand my mother's reaction.

"I know that. What is the meaning of this kind of garbage?"

I started to cry then. Mom grabbed the note from me and turned away. "I hope she has not been telling everyone all of this. What will they all think?"

As far as I know, Medhya never showed any inclination to follow through on the threats in the note. Sitting here with Medhya now, I dig my nails into my palm. I know that Medhya's right, in a way. Mom did seem to care more about appearances than about her daughter's mental health.

I turn to Medhya. "Was that why you stopped getting good grades in eleventh grade?"

She picks little pills of yarn off the afghan and tosses them onto the carpet. "I just didn't want to play that game anymore. They wanted me to get good grades, so I could get a degree in some prestigious field. Medicine, law, engineering. Then Mom could brag to her friends about how well I was doing, what a nice house I had. I was sick of the whole thing. So I engaged in a little civil disobedience." She smiles triumphantly.

"Well, all you did was hurt yourself, Medhya. Once you got to college, why didn't you just major in what you wanted? And why are you still trying to make Mom and Dad upset with you? You're not a kid anymore. You're just ruining your life." I'm surprised that I'm challenging her like this. I ought to be trying to soothe her.

"You act like I'm doing it on purpose." She shifts herself further under the afghan. Her lips are dry and cracked, and her eyes look dull, as though she has a fever.

If she's not doing it on purpose, who's forcing her? "You're almost 27, Medhya. You can study anything you want. You can do whatever you want. Why don't you do it?"

She sighs and looks at me pathetically. "That's what I've been trying to figure out all these years. What do I really want? It's not that easy to untangle what's right for me, from the mess of anger, guilt, and other crap Mom and Dad unloaded on me."

"Oh, come on, Medhya. It wasn't that bad. Why don't you think about all the good things Mom and Dad did for us? They bought us a whole set of encyclopedias. Remember? They had us take swimming lessons and music lessons and painting lessons and tennis lessons. If there was a lesson to be had, we were taking it. Remember? They took us to India every two years. They took us on nice vacations every year. We saw New York City, Washington, D.C., the Grand Canyon, and Yellowstone National Park."

"Yeah, they spent money on us, but everything we did, they managed to take the enjoyment out of it. Remember that time we went to New York City? For some reason, Mom wanted to go to an Italian restaurant that had gotten five stars in her tour book. Dad insisted on going to McDonald's, because he said he wasn't going to pay that kind of money for a plate of noodles. They fought about that the entire trip. It was always like that. Mom wanted to do something to impress people, and Dad just wanted to be left alone."

I remember. We ended up going to McDonald's, but Mom refused to eat anything at all. Dad got an entire meal—Big Mac, fries, and a shake—and he insisted that Medhya and I order the same. Neither of us could finish our meals. First of all, it was way too much food, and second of all, we were so upset. Then, Dad got mad because we were wasting food. It was not a pleasant trip.

Why is Medhya bringing up all this now, right before Mom's birthday party? I don't want to remember all of this. Things have been fine, ever since Medhya left home, ever since I got married.

Mom planned a beautiful wedding for us, and helped decorate our house. In fact, she got all of our drapes custom-made in India, at a fraction of what it would have cost here in the U.S.

Dad and I don't talk a whole lot, but he gets along great with Sandeep. They're always sitting around talking about Indian politics or the baseball scores. Nowadays, a lot of times, we really are a happy family. Sure, we've had some bad times, but why remember that now?

The only sad spot in our lives is Medhya. Every time she sees me, Mom asks me about Medhya. She has given up trying to call or email Medhya, because Medhya never calls back or replies. Whenever we talk about Medhya, Mom presses her lips together. I've never, ever seen my mother cry. She's proud of the fact that she never cries, but whenever we talk about Medhya, she looks like she might be about to cry.

"Why did you even come here, Medhya?" I whisper. "You haven't seen Mom and Dad in years, and when you walked into the house tonight, you wouldn't even talk to them. Mom made those *dosas* just for you. Why are you here?"

"The only reason I came here is for you, Vineeta. I didn't want to stay away and hurt you. You're one of my best friends, you know that?"

My immediate reaction is that I want to shout at her. Does she think she's doing me a favor by coming here and acting like a stranger?

Whenever Medhya tells me what a great sister I am, I feel like that's such a crock. Can't she see the truth? If I'm such a good sister, why do I mostly want to yell at her? A lot of times I don't even want to open her emails. I don't want to hear all the bad news I know she's going to dump on me.

"You're a really good listener," she continues.

I'm not a good listener. The only reason I haven't challenged Medhya in the past is that I'm afraid of hurting her. She's always seemed so fragile to me—like she could break at the slightest harsh word. She always seems in such bad shape that I didn't want my words to send her into a tailspin. So, I just sit there with the phone to my ear as she pours out her tales of woe.

But is she fragile? Maybe Medhya's just a stubborn, controlling person. Maybe the real reason I've been silent is that I've been afraid she'd hurt me with her scorching anger. A spineless sap is what I am.

Whenever she calls me on the phone, my heart sinks. I know it's going to be an hour-long conversation full of whining and self-pity. Many times, I've thought about yelling at her and hanging up, but I've never done that. The most I've done is tell her I can't talk right then, and not call her back. Is that what a good sister would do?

"Come upstairs with me." She pushes the afghan away and stands up. She seems suddenly energized. "I want to show you something."

I follow her upstairs. The bedroom smells of incense. I sit down on the bed.

Medhya is standing beside the dresser. I see a bunch of little statues on top of the dresser. They look like the goddesses we learned about in a women's studies class I once took. There are about five of them: a woman with incredibly wide hips who is supporting her breasts in her hands; a topless woman wearing a layered skirt and holding up two snakes; a gold-colored woman with green wings and a horned hat; a three-headed figure wearing Greek robes; and a Chinese-looking woman sitting cross-legged. I notice an incense holder with a half-burned stick among the bunch.

Medhya cups one of the goddesses in both her hands, like it's a delicate animal or something. She smiles mysteriously. "This is Ishtar," she says. It's the woman with the enormous hips. She sets Ishtar down carefully and picks up the three-headed one. "This is Hecate, the Triple Goddess."

"I didn't know you were interested in goddesses," I say. I find the statues kind of embarrassing. If I saw these in a museum, I'd be fine with them. Maybe what I'm embarrassed about is my sister's weird devotion to these pieces of stone, or plaster, or whatever they're made out of. Is this another one of her short-lived fads? "I thought you weren't into religion," I say. When we were kids we sat through hours and hours of Hindu *pujas*. We'd both gotten sick of that whole thing, I thought.

"Not Mom and Dad's kind."

"So what kind is this, then? Mom has lots of little god and goddess statues on her altar. You even have incense, just like Mom."

"This is about spirituality. It's not about mindless rituals like Mom and Dad do. I joined this women's group. We meet once a month, at the full moon. We do some chanting, depending on what we're working on in our lives. We bring offerings, like flowers or fruit, to the goddess who can help us with that."

"Sounds exactly like what Mom does."

"Well, it's not, Vineeta. Not at all. This is about women's independence and strength. The real issue is that men hate women." Her voice grows louder. "That's become completely obvious to me. And you know why? It's because we're powerful. In our group we explore primal female energy. We're the ones who are really connected to the universal life forces, Vineeta. It's not about penis envy. It's about the envy of giving life. That's women's power. That's why men have been trying to keep us down for centuries. They're jealous of our life-giving power."

She's just about shouting. Then, she looks at me and suddenly stops. Her expression is concerned. She must have seen something in my face.

I'm thinking about whether I really have that power to give life.

"I thought you might understand, Vineeta," she says, more gently.

I shake off my worry and nod, like I'm trying to understand. I know she'll probably give up this interest in a couple of weeks or months and flit on to something else—another boyfriend—like she's done all her life.

* * *

On Saturday morning, our reunion officially starts. Today, we're having a picnic at Hudson Springs Park.

"What about ice? I don't think we have ice!" Mom is scurrying around, trying to act like things are totally normal, as if she's not disturbed at all that her younger daughter has basically not spoken to her.

Medhya spent yesterday out, somewhere. Sandeep was picking people up from the airport. I was doing some last-minute cooking and shopping.

It's nine in the morning. Mom has already wrapped herself in a printed cotton *sari* and made up her face with powder, red lipstick, black eye-liner, and a large red *kumkum* in the middle of her forehead, but she looks haggard. I can tell she's upset.

"Dad and Murli Uncle went out to get the ice," I tell her, trying to be soothing. I'm peeling mangos for our fruit salad and handing each slippery orange fruit to my cousin Saumya, the one with the new five-bedroom house, who's slicing the mangos into cubes. Saumya's wearing a pretty green and gold *salvar kameez*. She is managing to keep her long, dangling sleeves out of the way of the mango juice on the cutting board. I'm also wearing a nice *salvar kameez* with an apron over it. I feel sick to my stomach.

Outside on the deck, the men are sitting around and talking. Saumya's kids are on the lawn, throwing a frisbee back and forth. Mom goes down to the basement to find another cooler.

Medhya appears silently at my side. I drop the peeler.

"Sorry," she whispers. "Didn't mean to startle you."

Medhya's wearing a new-looking pair of jeans and a pretty blouse. She looks OK—better than yesterday, certainly. I didn't expect her to wear Indian clothes. She probably doesn't even own any Indian outfits.

"Medhya," Saumya exclaims, putting her knife down, rinsing and drying her hands, and turning towards my sister with open arms. "Long time no see."

"Hi, Saumya. Great to see you, too." Medhya smiles politely and gives Saumya a little pat on the back.

Mom appears, carrying a dusty red cooler. "I found it!" She stops in her tracks when she sees Medhya.

I hold my breath.

Medhya nods in Mom's direction. "Oh, hi," she says. She slides her hands into the back pockets of her jeans.

I stand there dumbly. Saumya reaches for the cooler. "Let me take that, Auntie," she says smoothly, whisking it out of Mom's hands and onto the counter.

Mom has collected herself enough to put on a bright smile. "How are you, Medhya?"

Medhya shrugs. She takes something out of her pocket and holds it out to Mom. It's a small white paper package.

"What is this?" Mom accepts it with both hands, feigning surprise as though it isn't her birthday.

Mom unwraps the package—the wrapping is just a paper bag folded up—and Medhya escapes through the sliding glass doors onto the deck.

Mom lifts out a tan macrame bracelet with one pale pink stone attached. It's the kind of thing teenagers like to wear. Mom forces a smile of delight, but then noticing that I'm the only one looking at her—Saumya has turned politely back to the cutting board—Mom wraps up the bracelet and shoves it into the kitchen junk drawer.

* * *

We take a caravan of cars to Hudson Springs Park, where we have a shelter reserved. Medhya rides in the car with Sandeep and me.

"Did Mom like her present?" Medhya asks breathlessly, as we hum down the road.

I turn to look at her in the back seat. Her eyebrows are raised. She is smiling expectantly.

"Medhya, it's macrame. Mom doesn't wear macrame."

"It's handmade," Medhya insists. "A woman in my spirituality group makes them. The stone is rose quartz. It represents forgiveness. I'm working on forgiving Mom."

I open my mouth. I'll just make things worse by saying what's on my mind. I turn to face front again. How can Medhya even imagine that Mom needs her forgiveness? And couldn't she have thought of a more appropriate gift? OK, so she doesn't have much money, but even a beautiful handwritten card would have been better.

My stomach is in a knot by the time we get to the park. Medhya helps us carry the stuff to the shelter—the fruit salad, trays of lemon rice, yogurt rice, raw vegetables, a pot of chick pea curry, bottles of juice and pop, a coffee maker, plastic containers of *burfi* and brownies, and the charcoal.

As soon as everyone else arrives, Arvind and Sandeep take over the grill. We've got chicken patties for people who eat meat, and corn-on-the-cob for those who don't. Medhya heads down to the lake. I see her loping away with her skinny arms swinging. I assume that she'll be back, but she keeps on going around the lake. Soon she's just a tiny figure far along the path.

I don't know how I feel about her disappearance. On the one hand, as I'm arranging the food, encouraging people to eat, and laughing at Arvind's imitation of one of our uncles, I'm glad she's not around to make Mom uncomfortable.

On the other hand, can't she be normal and sociable for once? I keep looking out towards the lake, hoping I'll see her coming towards us, hoping she'll do the right thing and make our mother happy.

But she doesn't reappear. Everyone asks me, "How's Medhya doing in Newark?"

What can I say? I don't want to tell them about her job situation. I figure that's her news to share if she wants to. So, I roll my eyes and say something like, "Same as usual," or, "You know Medhya."

We laugh together.

I feel like a traitor for laughing about Medhya's reputation.

After the picnic, Medhya's waiting by our car. She's sitting on the curb and eating a brown square of something out of a plastic baggie. My whole head itches when I see her. I want to throw something heavy at her.

She stuffs her baggie into her pocket and stands up, reaching out to me. I let her take the cooler, which she silently places in the trunk of the car.

When we get home, Medhya heads directly upstairs. Everyone else sits around, on the deck and in the family room, talking and talking, laughing and laughing. Even my dad seems to be having a good time. Arvind organizes a group hike to Buttermilk Falls. We set out the picnic leftovers for supper. Saumya puts her kids to sleep on the fold-out couch in the basement. Mom brings out a deck of cards.

Even at two in the morning, when I drag myself upstairs, Mom is still talking with a few people. Their laughter follows me up the stairs.

Medhya's already in bed, asleep. Her breathing is even.

I lie down on top of the covers. I need to brush my teeth and change my clothes. I'm too exhausted to move.

Medhya hasn't closed the curtains. The moonlight glares in.

Just as I've decided to get up, Medhya starts rustling around.

"Wow. Look at Goddess Moon," she says thickly. She yawns and props herself up on her elbow, so that she can see out the window.

I jump up and pull the curtains closed. In the darkness, I find my toothbrush and head to the bathroom.

Medhya drops her head onto the pillow again.

I can't sleep. Tomorrow is the big birthday luncheon. Did I order enough appetizers? Will anyone get annoyed about the seating arrangements? Maybe I should have ordered another meat dish.

Medhya puts a hand on my shoulder. "Vineeta," she whispers, "you worry too much. Don't worry."

How does she know I'm worried? I must have been tossing around in the bed. Anyway, it's easy for her to tell me not to worry. She hasn't helped out at all.

"If you want, I can teach you a really powerful breathing technique," she offers. "It's great for relaxation."

"No, thanks." I roll away from her and curl myself into a ball at the edge of the bed.

* * *

It's Sunday morning. I corner Medhya as she comes out of the shower and into the bedroom, her head wrapped in a towel.

"You're not going to duck out of this lunch, are you?"

She puts her shampoo and soap box into her backpack. "I'll be there."

"What're you going to eat? You can't bring your own food into a restaurant."

"I'll eat salad, if they have it."

"Maybe I can order you a mango *lassi*. That's raw."

"I don't do dairy. But don't worry about me. I'll be fine."

"I have you sitting at the same table with Saumya's family. Be sociable, will you?"

"Don't worry, Vineeta."

Things seem to go fine during the meal. Every once in a while, I glance over at Medhya. She has seated herself between Saumya's children, a girl of six and a boy of eight, and is talking seriously with them. Fine. If she won't talk to adults, at least she can be useful in keeping the kids entertained.

While the birthday cake is being served, there are a bunch of toasts to my mother. We've set up a little podium with a microphone for this purpose. My stomach is in turmoil. Would Medhya dare to make a toast? And if so, what could she possibly say?

Radha Auntie, Mom's younger sister, stands up and tells everyone how Mom was like a mother to her. "She is six years older than me. Many older sisters would not want to be seen with their younger sister, but Sudha let me follow her around, when she was with her friends. She took me to the store, when she had an errand to do for our mother. She helped me with my homework. I think the saddest day of my life was the day Sudha got married and left home."

Radha Auntie starts crying as she tells this story.

I had no idea Mom was such a wonderful big sister. I look over at Mom at the next table and see that she's pressing her lips together, the way she does when she doesn't want to cry.

Next, Murli Uncle, Mom's brother from California, tells everyone how competitive Mom was as a kid. "She's younger than me and a girl besides, but she had to do everything my friends and I did. She insisted on learning to ride a bike. She played marbles with us. And, she had to win at everything. Fortunately, our mother made her stop playing with us by the time she turned eight or nine. Otherwise, she would have taken up cricket and put all the boys to shame."

Everyone laughs at this. I never realized Mom used to play with her brother and his friends. She has always seemed very feminine to me. Mom's trying not to laugh too much, but she looks pleased at this memory.

Then, various other relatives stand up and say the usual things—some funny, some touching. My father even takes a turn. He can't prevent himself from taking a dig at her. "Sudha and I have had our differences over the years, but one thing I can say—She is just as beautiful as the day I married her." Everyone laughs and hoots. My mother pretends to swat at my father's words.

What he said is not exactly a compliment, because one of the things my father criticizes my mother for is spending too much time and money on hair dyes, make-up, facials, diet products, clothing, jewelry, and so forth.

"He won't be happy until I look just as gray-haired, fat, and wrinkled as he is," she's always saying.

Finally, everyone shouts for me to come up to the microphone. I manage to say something bland and soothing about how my mother is my best friend, and how I'm proud to be her daughter. I watch Medhya, as I speak. Is the crowd going to insist that she come up here?

As I leave the podium, I hear shouts. "Medhya, you're next!"

My cousin Arvind walks over to her seat and pretends to haul her up to the podium. Medhya hunches in her chair and shakes her head. Arvind is persistent. The crowd's shouts grow louder.

I duck into my chair. Sandeep seems oblivious to the entire drama. He's happily eating his cake.

Medhya looks up and catches my eye. Finally, she stands and brushes Arvind away. She walks to the podium.

This is the moment I've been dreading. Most relatives know that Medhya hasn't had a good relationship with my parents, but I don't think anyone at the reunion realizes that Medhya has not said more than a few words to my mother, since she arrived.

The room is dead silent. Medhya stands there. Mom is pale and still.

Medhya looks at me. "I want to thank my sister for organizing this party." Her voice is even and calm. She turns to our mother and says, "Mom, happy birthday." She steps back from the microphone. Well, that wasn't so bad. It wasn't exactly good, especially after all the other toasts, but it could have been a lot worse.

Then she steps forward again and, leaning into the microphone, says in a louder, hurried voice, "I know I haven't been a very good daughter to you. I want you to know that I love you. I appreciate you for being independent. You're a strong woman, and I hope I can be half as strong as you are. I want to have the inner conviction that you have."

Medhya pauses. I look at Mom. She doesn't seem to know how to react. Isn't this just like Medhya to make an amazing speech, but in public? She knows Mom always wants to look appropriate and dignified in front of others. How is Mom supposed to react when her younger daughter, whom she hasn't spoken to in six years, comes up with a speech like this in public?

Medhya leaves the podium and walks towards Mom's table. The room is completely silent. Mom fumbles with the napkin in her lap. She attempts to stand up, but then sits back down.

Medhya reaches Mom's seat and holds out both hands to Mom. Medhya lifts Mom to her feet and gives her a big hug. A few people start clapping softly, but for the most part the room is silent.

Medhya pulls away.

Mom tries to flash a bright smile around the room, but I can see she's on the verge of tears. She presses her lips together hard, then ducks her head. Radha Auntie hands her a tissue, and she wipes her eyes. She sits back down. My aunt stands up and motions for Medhya to sit down in her place, which Medhya does.

The meal is over then, and so is the reunion. I look at Sandeep. "Life is full of surprises," he says. People are milling around. "Go and say good-bye to everyone," he reminds me. In shock, I take up my station near the door to thank everyone for coming. Mom and Medhya continue to sit at the table. A few people lean over to wish Mom one final happy birthday.

Relatives stream past to thank me for the reunion. Most of them make no reference to Medhya's astonishing speech. I suppose they don't know what to think. They give me hugs and say things like, "When will you come to see us?"

Only Radha Auntie says, "I hope this is a turning point for them," nodding towards the table where Mom and Medhya are sitting.

By the time Sandeep and I leave, Medhya and Mom are still sitting together, talking. We take Dad with us, so Mom will have the car.

In the car, Dad says, "I told Sudha not to get her hopes up. It will never last."

I have a throbbing headache. Every bone in my body feels exhausted. I go directly upstairs and lie down.

Sandeep says he'll be back to pick me up, later.

Dusk falls outside, as I lie on the bed.

I hear the door open. "You're awake," Medhya murmurs.

"Hmm." I don't move.

Medhya moves around the darkened room, quietly.

The bed sags, as she sits down beside me. "Here. This is Ishtar. I want you to have her."

I open my eyes and see Medhya holding out one of her goddess figures—the one with the platter hips.

I don't reach for it. "What for?"

"She's a fertility goddess. I thought she might help you." She pauses. "To have a baby. Mom told me you're having a hard time." When I still make no move to take the goddess, Medhya reaches for my hand and presses the figurine into my palm.

"Mom told you that?" I struggle against my fatigue to sit up.

Medhya nods. "Mom's really worried about you."

"She shouldn't be." I put the statue on the bed and stand up. I don't want Medhya's pity. I drag my suitcase out from under the bed. I may as well start packing my clothes, so I'll be ready when Sandeep arrives. I have to be at work early tomorrow morning.

"Well, you know Mom. Her hobby is worrying about her daughters. Anyway, it worked out well in the end. If Mom hadn't been so worried about you, she never would have agreed to this."

"What do you mean?"

"The only reason she agreed to let you plan this reunion is that she thought it would help you get your mind off trying to get pregnant. Isn't that crazy? I mean, she resisted the idea for so long, and as it turned out, she had a great time."

No thanks to you, I can't help adding silently.

As though reading my mind Medhya says, "I'm sorry I didn't help you plan the reunion, Vineeta. You really put in a lot of work. You did a great job."

I nod and try to smile. I had no idea that Mom was using the reunion as a sort of therapy for me. I'm not the daughter who needs therapy. "It's no big deal, really." I shrug. "I'm sure everything will work out fine. I mean, we can always go to India and adopt."

"You have such a good attitude, Vineeta." Medhya says this sincerely. "Mom made it sound like you were pining away with sorrow."

I don't know what to say to this. I sit back down on the bed. I feel weird that Mom and Medhya have been talking about me behind my back. Medhya's the one who has hard times—not me. I'm the one who laments about my sister with my mother.

I place the statue facing away from me on the nightstand next to the bed. I have no idea what I'll do with it. Maybe I'll just "forget" to take it home. Medhya will never know.

Or maybe I should give the little statue back to Medhya. She probably doesn't realize what she's doing, giving away something she seems to treasure. She probably doesn't realize how much she'll miss it. She's the one who cares about it, at least right now, while she's in her goddess phase.

I change the subject. "So, how long did you guys stay at the restaurant?"

"We left pretty soon after you did, but then we went to the coffee shop next door. We just got back."

"Hmm." I nod slowly. "So you and Mom are friends now?" I ask this cautiously. This is something I've wanted for so long—one big happy family. It's like I've been handed something precious and fragile, and I don't want to break it.

Medhya smashes it out of my hands right away. "No. Not really."

She gets up off the bed and looks out the window. "Hello, moon," she says. Then, turning back to me, "I mean, when I first sat down with her, it was great to talk to her after so long. I really thought I could turn over a new leaf, you know? But towards the end of the afternoon, she was starting to say those same old things that drive me crazy. I don't know how you deal with it, Vineeta."

"What did she say?" I feel a twisting in my gut.

I know what I'm going to hear—a litany of old complaints.

Medhya is now sitting on the floor beside the dresser, packing up her goddesses in the dark. "Oh, you know," she says, without looking at me. "Now that I'm unemployed, she wants me to move in with her and Dad and finish college. Can you imagine living with Mom and Dad again? I'd go bonkers."

I walk to the light switch and flip it on. "Well, I guess it's nice of them to offer. You know, Indian parents always want their kids to live with them."

"Sure. On their terms. I can just hear it now. 'Don't stay out too late. Why are you hanging out with that guy? It's not too late to go to medical school.'

"And of course, I'd have to hear their arguments. She'd complain to me about his slobby habits and his lack of desire to do anything at all, and he'd complain to me about how she's always spending his money to impress people."

I sigh. "Anyway, you can still go back to college, even if you don't want to live with Mom and Dad."

"Don't start that, Vineeta."

I look at the white figure on the nightstand. I have a sudden urge to fling it to the ground and stomp on it. I take a deep breath. "Does this mean you're not going to speak to Mom and Dad anymore? Was that all for show—what you did at the luncheon today?"

She flips her hair away from her face and looks at me. "The only reason I stood up and spoke today was for you, Vineeta. I didn't want to ruin the celebration you planned. I didn't even realize I was going to make up with Mom. It just happened.

"I don't want to live with her, but Mom and I decided we'll talk every few weeks. I think I can handle her in small doses."

I watch her putting away the goddesses. She seems compulsive about them. She wraps each one with a square of silk cloth. Then, she places them all into a zippered pouch embroidered with Chinese-looking plants and birds. As she finishes with the last one, she takes a breath and lets out a theatrical sigh. "Well, back to my wonderful life in Newark."

"If you don't like it, why don't you leave, now that you don't have a job?" This comes out sounding harsher than I'd meant it to. I guess I'm still hurt that Medhya and Mom have been talking about me behind my back.

"My lease doesn't run out until the end of the year." She's doing her monotone "depressed" voice again.

"Can't you sublet?"

"This is Newark we're talking about, Vineeta. Who wants to sublet an ugly apartment in Newark?"

For the second time this weekend, I have the urge to shake her by the shoulders. I feel like giving up on her, telling her off, and putting her out of my life, but of course, I'd never do that.

"Do you need help? I'd be happy to lend you some money, since you have no savings." I try not to say this in an accusing way, but why didn't she save any of the money she's earned?

She stands up and gives me a stony stare. "I don't believe in using money earned through the military."

At first I have no idea what she's talking about. Then, I realize that this is a reference to Sandeep's job. He's a software consultant to a company that has some contracts with the military.

This makes me so angry that I'm speechless. Here I am, offering to lend her money without consulting Sandeep, because I'm sure he'd be fine with helping his sister-in-law, and all she can do is insult him.

I feel an itch all over me. I have to say something. "You came here planning to ignore Mom, didn't you?" My voice rises to a shout. "You came here planning to ruin things. You've been ruining our family for years. Mom's the one who should be forgiving you. What kind of a daughter are you?" I can't believe I'm saying this. Any of our relatives might be in the house. Anyone could hear me.

I regret the words as soon as I say them. I don't know what kind of reaction to expect from Medhya. I feel myself shrinking up inside, like a slug with salt poured on it.

But Medhya starts to smile. In fact, she starts to laugh. "You've changed, Vineeta," she says softly. "You've really been speaking your mind these last couple of days. Good for you."

This makes me even angrier. She's turning the tables, pretending there's been something wrong with me all these years. She's the one who's been messing everything up, not me. "Why?" I scream. "Why are you like this?

"Mom's hurting too. She just tries not to show it. She's grown this hard shell from being around Dad all the time. And even when you stopped speaking to her, she kept on going. You, you're no help at all. You're a walking disaster."

Medhya opens her mouth as if to say something. Instead, she turns away from me, flings the backpack over her shoulder, and opens the door.

I watch her go. The scene plays out, as if in slow motion. This isn't the way I want the reunion to end.

At the doorway, she stops and glances back at me. I don't know what she sees in my face, but she steps into the room again and sets her backpack down.

She walks over to me. I'm afraid she might slap me. Instead, she puts an arm around me. "You're totally stressed," she murmurs. "Lie down." She leads me to the bed and pulls back the bedspread. I sink onto the mattress, and she covers me up.

I close my eyes. The yellow light overhead pierces my eyelids. Then, darkness. Medhya has turned off the light.

I feel strange. I feel like what I've wanted for so long— a happy family—is floating off into thin air. Not the happiness part, but the image I've held in my mind of what a happy family should be.

My eyelids flutter. Medhya's hand rests lightly on the blanket, and the moonlight lays a band of silver across the bed. The house is quiet. I'm so exhausted that my mind is whirling along crazy, incomprehensible paths. I know if I don't hold on tight, I might drift away from the life I've been living. I remind myself to hold on, but I have the sense that, if I relax my vigilance, I might just let go and glide.

Alexander Weinstein

REINCARNATIONS OF SPACE-MEN

This past summer, I managed to make my son afraid of death and astronauts in one fell swoop.

Peter and I were visiting my parents for the month. This was to be the first time, since the separation, that I would have Peter for an extended period of time—four weeks to be exact.

We'd driven from Michigan to Massachusetts. Peter was doing amazingly well with the separation.

His mother called every night to check in. On this particular night, she told me about the death of her great-aunt.

She may have told Peter about this too, or perhaps Peter overheard me mentioning the death to my parents.

It was a summer night. I was trying to sing Peter to sleep. As I lay next to my son in the bed, I was suddenly presented with Peter's first question about death.

The question took me by surprise. Peter was three. I hadn't expected to tackle this subject until much later. I'd imagined that the death conversation would come up around age six or seven. Perhaps I was hoping I'd have more answers by then.

Holding my son, I realized we were sharing a crucial moment—one wherein my boy, who must have been turning the idea of death around in his head for hours, now ventured to ask me about one of life's unanswered mysteries.

As a parent, you feel the power of landmark moments. These are the moments when you teach your child how to spin a coin, or demonstrate the laws of gravity. Here, however, the stakes were high. I would be the first influence in shaping my son's perception of death.

At first, I attempted a bit of a dodge. I asked Peter what he thought happened when someone dies.

He told me, quite simply, that he didn't know. He asked me again to explain.

My parents are not particularly religious. They raised me with the freedom to pursue whatever religion I wished. My leanings have been predominantly Buddhist and Taoist, philosophies that believe in an immutable universal energy. They include some form of reincarnation in their discussions of death. It was these beliefs that I wished to instill in my son, not the anxieties of heaven and hell, eternal damnation, or atheistic beliefs of nothingness.

All the same, as I began to answer Peter's question, I felt it unfair to present him solely with the Eastern model. For this reason, I presented my three-year-old son with a philosophical overview of death.

"Well," I began, "some people believe there's something called heaven." I gave a brief synopsis of clouds and gates. "Then," I explained, "some people think there's nothing when you die." I put as little credence as possible to this depressing view of death. Finally, I explained Buddhist notions of reincarnation. "In essence," I told him, "nobody really knows what happens. There are a lot of different ideas about it."

Peter was wide awake, as we lay in darkness. "What do you think, Papa?"

"Here's what I like to believe," I told him. "When we die, our energy, some call it soul, becomes part of the universe. All of the universe—the air, the stars, the moons, and the planets—is sustained by souls in transition, between lives.

"When we die, we do mighty things. We travel through galaxies, or we enter the realms of gods. There are infinite possibilities.

"At some point, we are called back to earth. There is something we are meant to do on this planet, so we return as babies."

This is a working hypothesis, and I presented it as such. At the time, Peter seemed to like the theory.

For the last weeks of June, the question of death became a nightly topic. Peter and I would lie in bed, discussing theories of the afterlife like ancient philosophers, like old friends in this cycle of incarnations. Perhaps, we'd done this thousands of years ago, he my father and I his son, he my teacher and I his student, both of us wizened Taoists sitting by a waterfall.

Soon, the month ran its course. Our time together came to an end. I flew back with my boy to Michigan and said goodbye to him. It would be another month, until I saw him again.

* * *

Recently, I picked Peter up for our first weekend together, since our summer trip. During the drive, Peter presented me with his interpretation of my afterlife philosophy.

Apparently, he'd been processing the subject of death, since I'd last seen him.

"Do you want to go to outer space?" Peter asked.

"Sure," I said. "Who knows. Maybe when you're my age, you'll be able to take trips to outer space." I thought we were talking about good-old-astronaut stuff.

"Am I going to have to go to outer space?" Peter wanted to know.

"No, only if you want to. Astronauts go out into space all the time."

"I don't like astronauts."

"Why not?"

"Because when you go to outer space, you die."

And there it was. I had, in attempting to give my son a holistic view of death, utterly frightened him. I had frightened him not merely of dying but of outer space—the sun, the moon, the stars, the darkness, the night, and astronauts.

Astronauts. Kids usually love astronauts. As far as Peter was concerned, however, those strange men were heading towards their death, when they blasted off. In a consequent turn of logic, he had figured out that he and I could avoid death, if we never boarded a spaceship.

I tried to explain the difference between astronauts and the philosophies I'd told him. I discounted my own half-formed theories as *just an idea your papa thinks*. "Who knows what really happens?" I said.

It was no use. He was frightened.

As a father, I want to make life easy for Peter. I want to explain the unexplainable. I want to allay his fears with wisdom that, truthfully, I don't yet have.

I have no clue what happens, when we die. On a plane, I still grip the armrests, silently praying to be kept alive, when we hit turbulence. In the end, I am simply Peter's father, a human being prone to the same fears, failings, and insecurities as everyone else. This may seem like an obvious realization, yet all fathers share the hope of being infallible—to be more than the sum of one's history.

Fatherhood, however, is a process of learning. It is not a fixed state of wisdom. This implies that we will make mistakes.

* * *

Last Halloween, through unintentional coincidence, I ended up mitigating Peter's fear of outer space.

I was dressed up as a "space guy."

Peter was a pirate. He seemed to find great relief in seeing that I was a space guy and still alive. He tried on my costume several times. Then, we went through his toys.

"Turn this one into a space guy," he said, picking up a Playmobil pirate.

I made a *woo-woo-woo* sound, and the pirate became a space man.

"Turn the T-Rex into a space guy," Peter urged me, putting the dinosaur into my hand.

Woo-woo-woo.

We spent the next hour turning all his Playmobil figures and stuffed animals into space people.

Then, in the quiet of our small apartment, we turned them back into toys again.

Frederick J. Sievert

A BUSINESS LESSON FROM DAD

The entire family was driving back from the two-week visit with my ailing father, when we received the call telling us he had passed away. The news was not unexpected.

Dad's own testimony to us before his death about the love and bright beauty of the other side had given us courage. He had experienced a near death transcendence into the world beyond and was eagerly awaiting his own final passage.

After receiving the news of his passing, we drove the rest of the way home. There, we unpacked, repacked, and caught a flight back to Michigan, to deal with the funeral arrangements.

Little did I know that, on this return visit, God had other very important messages to deliver to me, lessons that greatly increased my appreciation for my father and enriched my management style.

As I began to look through my dad's personal files, I came across a sheaf of notes that he'd received while still working as an insurance inspector. The notes were short, simple expressions of appreciation from his superiors. There was often nothing more than a handwritten message that said, "Fred—nice job on this case." These small discoveries amongst his belongings triggered an array of thought and emotion in me.

As I sat and stared at the pile of messages, images of Dad working so hard day and night for his family came to mind. He was an insurance inspector by day, but he also played the trumpet professionally in the evenings. I realized in that instant that I had inherited my work ethic from him. The family meant everything to him, and he worked hard, very hard, to make life as comfortable as possible for Mom, my brother Rob, and me. Suddenly, I appreciated how much he had sacrificed for us.

Dad was a smart man. He could converse intelligently with almost anyone on any topic, but he lacked a formal education. He had been forced to work to support his own family as a child during the Great Depression.

He excelled at playing the trumpet. That great passion became a source of modest income to supplement his tedious day job.

The only real break Dad took from work was to attend sporting events, to watch his two boys play. That gave him great joy.

I only remember one family vacation.

I recalled many of these long-forgotten scenes, as I sat poring over Dad's papers.

Dad was a man of faith. He didn't have a church or a house of worship. Nonetheless, we knew he believed.

Dad never drank and often stated proudly how many years it had been since his last drink. I don't think he had ever been an alcoholic. My impression was that he simply recognized the evils of excessive drinking and didn't want to risk falling into that trap. He had too much work to do to support his family.

At that moment I thanked the Lord for giving me these rapid-fire flashbacks of my years with Dad. They had gone by so quickly, and I hadn't told him often enough how much I loved and appreciated him.

I returned to the task at hand. As I read and reread many of the short notes, I realized how easy, quick, and meaningful a simple expression of praise or appreciation can be. My dad had saved these notes over many years. He had probably reviewed them throughout his retirement.

At the time of Dad's death, I was an Executive Vice President at New York Life. I managed the company's largest business unit, with over ten thousand agents and four thousand employees. Although I had only eight or ten executives reporting directly to me, I knew hundreds of employees and agents personally. It occurred to me how infrequently I thanked them for a job well done. On those occasions when I had thanked them or written them a note, I wondered how many of them, like my dad, might have created a file of such complimentary notes from the boss.

I thanked the Lord and my dad for reminding me of that simple management tip. As a result of this revelation, I started a practice the following Christmas season. I sent annual holiday greeting cards to over three hundred New York Life employees. In each of these cards, I included a handwritten personal note of appreciation for their work. Since this was a time-consuming task, I started the process well before Thanksgiving, to make sure I'd get them all out before the Christmas holidays.

Years later, at a number of retirement parties held for me around the globe, I got misty-eyed, as so many people thanked me for what those cards meant to them. Many, including my successor, said that they had saved a file of those cards over the years.

I guess this shouldn't have surprised me, because of the lesson from Dad. Still, it struck me in a compelling and wonderful way.

But the Lord wasn't done yet. On the very same day that I discovered the file of messages in Dad's belongings, I was in a shopping mall, where I noticed a man who looked very familiar. He approached me and asked if I was Fred Sievert. It turns out that he was an employee named Alan Lauer. Alan had worked for me many years before, when I was an executive at Maccabees Mutual Life Insurance Company in Southfield, Michigan. He went on to say that his fondest memory of me was when I had called him after a presentation he made to our executive management committee, to express my appreciation, as well as my confidence in his knowledge and abilities. At that very moment, as a relatively new employee, he knew that he had chosen the right position, with the right company, with the right leadership.

What a wonderful and reassuring message this was for me to hear. How remarkable that it occurred only hours after I had discovered Dad's file of complimentary notes.

This could not be a coincidence. It was too timely and too improbable. We had returned to Michigan hundreds of times to visit family and friends over the years, and I had strolled through that same mall on nearly every trip. I had never once run into anyone I knew.

I think of these memories and happenings as gifts that helped me to deal with the grief of my loss. I thanked the Lord for reminding me of the importance of expressing appreciation to those who make a difference in our lives.

Noel Conneely

BREAKING EGGS

The sky had a look on its face
like yesterday's thunder
and father cracked the eggs
in the dim kitchen
as the branches at the window
played tricks with the light.
He whistled as the eggs fried.
Prayer was a taste
that stayed on the tongue
long after the priest's name
had slipped our minds.
Although as kids
we were avid God-eaters,
we preferred the breakfast
our dad prepared after Mass.
But someone called him out as he ate
and when he got back
the yellow had hardened on the plate.
He just mumbled something
and put it in the sink.

Eric Mothes

THE LITTLE BOY

He came from unprotected sex.
Unwanted from both sides, the little boy,
malnourished, manages his way
out of the massive hole his head is shaping.
He emerges to be thrown at the wide white wall
to the left of the waiting room. Hospitalized
for the next year, the little boy awakens all alone.
No parents, no relatives, no nothing;
just him and the nurses. Five years pass,
while he sits in a home.
People come to take him home.
There is no love in sight,
just corrupt check collectors
catering to their own selfish needs.
The little boy, isolated at school,
has no friends and overeats,
binges on bologna, butter, beef, brittle,
bacon, bread, brownies and biscuits.
Now fat and grotesque, he is even
more ridiculed. The little boy writes a note
saying, "Circle yes or no," and receives the reply,
"Hell, no!" *No* becomes familiar.
The little boy plays with nothing,
wears clothes too small for a younger child.
His already grim grades drop lower.
Schizophrenic now, he finds

his first friend in a rat he names Sam.
He tells his mom he loves her.
She laughs, so he takes it out on the rat,
slices Sam several times, leaving nothing
but a severed friend.
Like Mike Myers in *Halloween*
the little boy wears a mask,
but his is not literal. He uses it to hide
the hideous horror he has become.
Violence flows in his blood,
like the flood with Katrina,
like waves to the ocean,
like deaths from a serial killer.
The little boy, angry with the world,
has lost all sense of reality.
Name-calling, bad parenting, wrong timing;
we have created a monster,
the kind that wears trench coats
and starts the Columbine Massacre,
the kind that kills thirty-two people,
at two different times
during the Virginia Tech Massacre.
The little boy who committed social suicide
will soon take his own life.
Scared, he will first murder more.
He musters up strength.
He is down, dead, and demonic looking.
The police and parents ponder who is at fault.
The blame is precariously placed
on pointless topics that have no truth,

for the consequences were created.
We live once. Just once
help the little boy grow.

Eric Mothes

STEP DADDY

A crack head, a bum, a sadistic piece of shit,
a cruel corrupt fucking coward. These words alone are you.
The man most boys idolize, gone after astonishing abuse
is inflicted. Blood on the floor
mixes with tears. No one is moving but you.
You run as a ridiculous excuse of a man.
Years pass and only hatred builds in our souls.
I remember that day too well, while mom voids it.
I ain't small no more and need you for nothing,
but if you should come, this is what I'd tell you.
I remember that day you slammed
her head onto the stove. As she lay on the floor,
you stood alone above her talking shit.
I remember the big bulky bat you beat me with
'til I laid like a common corpse. I remember watching
through frightened foggy eyes
slightly blinded by a broken nose,
as you left. Crawling 'cause I could not stand,
I placed my body in the middle of the street.
My mom still not moving—
my only concern. All I could do was hope
someone would see me.
I remember all of it.

Then I would say some more.
After that day I filled

myself with furious vengeance.
Lunatics labeled me bipolar.
I took up the fearless family values you instilled,
belittling and beating.
I covered my body with blue tats—
some to cover the scary scars
and some to remind me of the horrors.
Look at my back and bent broken nose.
I spent several years wanting to kill you.
In jail I learned to let it go.
A big book called the *Bible*
had your name inscribed in it.
I shared the cell
where you did time.
I learned that living like I did
was me becoming you.
That scared me,
enough.

Daddy I saw you finally in a place
where I could not speak to you.
You were in a semi-old obituary.
It said you overdosed in jail.
On the lonely line next to you,
I left a comment.
Daddy, I hope our God,
glorious,
found you too.

Ines P. Rivera Prosdocimi

WHAT THE GODS DON'T DETERMINE

Mama & Papa buy me a cross.
That shiny silver capsule of God

makes me feel grown.
Spring's first sun, a drizzle of rain,

& we ride away from the cathedral,
ready to conserve our crosses & bones.

Papa tells me don't look
at a man running naked in the street.

A hand across my eyes doesn't keep me
from staring at that man's behind,

smooth and black like Papa's.
I don't hear the car horns or the woman

chasing after him. I hear the low humming
of the cathedral's walls, see that man

descend as the pigeons do
in colored light streaming down

from stain-glass windows to the ground.
At night, I bathe with my mother.

She tells of nine different angels
I can't see. I run my hand

over the white rolls of her stomach.
In a story book, I discover twelve more

Gods and not a single one looks like me.
They've told me I'm a mythological hybrid,

how my broad back misses its wings,
that the pigtails I wear are two horns

to defend myself, and if I go to sleep
hooves will replace my feet.

Next to a picture of my parents,
where Mama's hand rests on Papa's wool hair,

as he looks into her green eyes,
I set my cross down on the dresser.

M. Dobrovolsky

MONASTERY

An unmailed letter found among the possessions
of the late Father A——

My Dear Archbishop N——,

I am writing to you about a man, one of our own, who came here to the monastery from a faraway country some years ago. He accepted the terms and conditions of our life, declared himself a believer—a voluntary convert to Orthodoxy some years earlier—and stated his purpose for wishing to join our tiny community high above the sea.

"To be closer to God." That was all he said. The brothers and I decided to give him a trial period of six months. That has now stretched into three years, and he has become one of us.

He is humble, obedient, and honorable. Although he spoke little at first, he quickly fit in. He has always been ready to do his share of the work, and more. He told us that he had once worked in some sort of greenhouse or plant nursery, and offered his services to us in that area, which was most welcome. None of us had any complaints about him.

And yet as I watched, being the guardian of our community's spiritual life, I began to suspect that he was not truly engaged in our services, or in his prayers. There was an abstracted quality about his face as he sang, prayed, or even read aloud. I felt his sincerity at first, but later, his voice began to disturb me. I sensed a human sincerity, but—how shall I put this—no reaching out to the divine. He sounded as if he were reciting a work of literature, one that touched him and moved him. He did not, however, sound as if he were raising prayers to God.

I put it down to his coming late to the language of our catechism.

I cannot say that I felt this same gulf between his actions and our goals in other aspects of his life here. He is unfailingly polite. He stays away from the petty jealousies and squabbles that can emerge in such a tightly knit community. It was only his voice during our services that troubled me—his voice and his face.

I watched him carefully, whenever the opportunity presented itself. I saw strange things.

When, during the services, the deacon intoned the words "A prayer to God . . .," this man smiled. It was a light, gentle smile, but a distinctly mundane smile. The effect was disconcerting.

Please do not misunderstand me. I am not suggesting that there was anything strange in his smile itself.

I listened to his confessions when he took Communion. They were, to use the same word again, sincere but perfunctory. Over and over again, they were perfunctory.

Do not mistake my intentions, dear Archbishop. I do not expect of our people pained tirades about their unworthiness and lives of inner sin. Not at all. Still, many of our number will confess about their striving to be one with our Lord, and their falling short. They speak about their spiritual weaknesses and concerns, as well as confessions of the kind of pettiness that

I have alluded to above. They draw strength from Confession and Holy Communion.

But this man, how can I say it, appeared disturbingly self-contained. He seemed not so much in the state of spiritual peace that some brothers eventually manage to attain, but simply— again, words fail me—at ease with himself, as if he were not so much in a monastery as at some kind of secular retreat.

Even so, he wears the black robe and cross, and his beard has become shot with gray.

He tends the plants. This above all he does quietly and expertly, for hours on end, without haste, day after day. Unless I am mistaken, he sometimes holds a handful of herbs and talks to them, very quietly and very slowly.

Our gardens and decorative plants are all splendid, but not ostentatious. They are simple and quietly perfect, a reflection of the man.

At some point, I began to notice him observing me. Had he suspected that I was observing him? This went on for some months, until I noticed a change in his face. It seemed to me that he was catching my eye deliberately, in such a way that I might approach him to ask what was on his mind.

I decided that my actions had been unworthy, though well-meant. I stopped observing him at our services. Of course, our daily spoken communication continued, and as from the start, it was always respectful.

One warm day, I was sitting on a bench in the herb garden. I was absent in some sense from my body, transported by the blue of the sea so far below, the whiteness of our walls, the delicate greens of the garden, the beautifully placed stones, and the sound of bees. I felt close to our Lord in this place, which seems to be a reply to the Garden of Gethsemane. There, our Lord suffered betrayal, whereas this garden is a place of peace and truth.

When I emerged, the man of whom I have been speaking was sitting next to me. He sat calmly, with his hands on his knees. He turned to me and smiled gently, nodding in greeting.

I nodded back.

"So, dear Father A., shall we talk now?" he said. His quiet way startled me. He seemed to know all that had been passing though my mind these last few months.

At that moment, an airplane flew overhead, bound for the mainland. I composed myself and replied that I would talk about whatever he wished.

"But Father," he said. "Let us not speak in the code of our discipline. Let us speak as men."

I told him I did not understand what he meant.

"You do, I am sure," he said. "I do not wish to speak of a spiritual crisis, weak faith, unworthiness, or the like."
I confess that I was baffled at this. I asked him what he wished to speak about with me and whether it fell outside the boundaries of Confession.

"Perhaps," he said. "Perhaps not. I want to tell you about why I am here."

I told him that he had stated his desire—to be closer to God. Had he failed in this?

"Oh, no," he said, with a lightness in his voice. "I am no closer, but I am also no further from God than I have ever been."

I must have had a truly puzzled look on my face.

"First of all, Father, I must tell you that I don't believe in God or the dogma of our church."

I was thunderstruck.

"Please listen. When I came here, I said I wanted to be closer to God. Let me tell you how I meant to accomplish that. I don't believe in the God of the great religions. The loving, punishing, baffling, remote God who is both here and not here all at the same time. I believe that if there is a God—if—we must find him by simply being quiet, listening, and looking. Listening and looking around us. Not listening to the beauty of the stories and hymns and prayers and admiring the beauty of the church or our ancient traditions, not glorifying our relationship with Him or reciting His thousand and one names. Not with the endless prayer of a silent monastery. Just by shutting our traps and opening our eyes and ears."

I was rooted to the bench in silence.

He turned to me and smiled. "All we do to reach God, all the obedience, the prayers, the songs, the icons, the decorations, the beauty of the bells, and the calls to prayer—would you not agree that these are but poor approximations of the glory of God?"

I felt my face compressing. Its muscles were at war with each other. I wanted to nod in agreement, but I also wanted to show anger over where he was trying to lead me. I knew he wanted to go somewhere with his question, somewhere that I felt it unwise to go.

"The world is too much here, even here," he said looking around. "Only the mute plants and the bees are close to God."

"Why?" I asked.

"Because they do not think," he said. "They are perfect in their nature."

"You could live in a cave," I blurted out, "if you did not want this world, any world."

"I would still be human," he said. "And what makes us human separates us from God. He, I think, must be like a bee or a plant."

"Blasphemy." I stood up to leave him. "God is not simply nature."

He put his hand on my arm.

His touch soothed me. I sat down again.

"I had hoped to have a dialogue with you, Father. You are wise, and your soul penetrates mine. You saw that something was amiss. I could not disguise my innermost self from you. Do you want to know what is behind my wish to be closer to God?"

I waited a long time, before I nodded. It was my duty to this man's soul to deal with his error.

He turned to me and spoke earnestly. "What is it to be human? It is to have thoughts and ideas, to need love and support, to respond to the impulse to create, to move the objects of the mind into ever-new configurations."

"This is all true," I said. "I see nothing false about it."

He shook his head. "I am certain that all these are misleading distractions from our ability to be closer to God." He was quiet for a moment and turned to face the sea. Then, he said, "I came here to put down the burdens which lead us to wander in an immense and endless forest. Instead, I find all the same burdens."

"Of course," I said, "in the monastic life, we reduce these to a minimum, so we can focus on our relation to God and His Christ. Surely, you understand that."

"No, Father. This is not what we do. I have come to understand that we distract ourselves here, too. In fact, our distractions are not minimized, for we are to turn our energies to thinking of God, imagining Him, being lived by Him, relying on Him for support and strength. We are to create and recreate the word of the Gospels and the music of the divine services, to imagine and re-imagine His glories in our mind. We trouble our minds with Him incessantly. We recreate the outside world's distractions, piece for piece. We are not different from the secular world or the disciplines of the other religions, except in the object of our activity."

At this point, I began to fear for his soul.

"Are you searching for emptiness?"

He turned to me, smiling affectionately.

"Father, I am impressed."

I stifled a weak smile of pride and reminded him that we monks are not merely ignorant believers. We, too, had our struggles, before we accepted the truth of our belief.

"I am not rediscovering anything," he said. "The emptiness I seek is found everywhere."

"My son," I said, "it is precisely our activities here that lead us closer to God. It is that simple. We have turned our human faculties away from the vanities of the world and towards the glorification of God and His Son."

He looked at me with disappointment, as if he had expected more from me.

"Can I speak of the world?"

I said nothing. I could not.

He took this for consent. "At some point I realized this. Life in the world is a blank. All the daily efforts, work, socializing, schedules, results—all these things are gone once we act on them. Whatever we do fades from memory, even from our own memory. I looked back, and all I saw was a blank."

He paused, appearing to reconsider what he had said.

"Not all of it. My children are real, but they go their own ways. The rest of my efforts—our efforts—merely fill time. I know. I understand that through them we produce something called culture, but culture is an imaginary fortress in which we hide for fear of the vastness of the universe."

For a moment, I glimpsed what he meant. I had sometimes wondered whether I had come to the monastery to avoid confronting the world. His words, though, were more disturbing than that.

"Why do you stay here, if you believe that all you are doing is, as you might put it, filling time?"

"I'd expected the monastic life to be different, but as I've said, it is not. The daily activities here are also a blank. They are well ordered, perhaps, but restless and pointless. We pray to God. We read from holy books. We sing of Him and His angels. We ask Him to bless our food. We wake up in the darkness of morning to address Him. We ring bells to Him. We never give Him a moment's peace."

I laughed at this image. I could not help myself. He had touched upon something. How busy we keep ourselves.

He went on.

"This monastery is like the outside world in its restless activity, as if activity alone will obtain for us spiritual wealth, just as activity in the outside world will obtain material wealth. This is all I have found here—the same world, in effect. No, wait. Perhaps that is incorrect, because I have found something in the garden. I have found that nothing of which we spoke."

He smiled at the paradox and waved his hand at the sea.

"Out in the world, they are dimly aware of this. The stock trader, the car racer, the creative artist. They all speak of leaving their rational minds behind and operating on instinct at critical moments, but they are not truly living like this. Instead, those moments of release become like an addiction to them. They must repeat them again and again, like a person who is addicted to drugs, or to falling in love, or to sex.

I raised my hand when he said the word "sex." This was something I did not want to discuss.

He went on. "I'm not going to talk about sex, Father. I want to talk about love."

"Then go on," I said.

"I have experienced love many times, in many forms. Once, I experienced what I believe was real love. This may have happened, because I was old enough both to experience and understand it. Believe me when I say that it was carnal and transcendent at the same time. We reveled in our physical passion and yet loved each other with the same unselfish love that parents have for children. It was then that I began to see the world as it is."

"And what is the world as it is?" I asked, perhaps sarcastically.

"It is not what I'd expected. I began to lose interest in music, art, reading, and all the artificial creations of the masquerading brain. I was whole without them. Curiously, I began to write to express what I felt, not what my opinions were or what I was 'thinking.' My rational brain, that thin layer of neo-cortex that shrouds our most unselfconscious and intuitive processes, was finally at their service. And so I first saw the world as it really is only in adulthood. Do you know the perfection of a single leaf and how indifferent it is to its fate, or to yours or mine?"

He tends the plants so well, the silent plants, I thought.

"God loves you as a parent loves a child," I said. "His is the love of which you just spoke."

"He has a strange way of showing it," he replied. "He tells us that we must worship Him, of our own free will of course, and that we must submit voluntarily to His love or we will be punished eternally. What kind of strange love is this?"

I was silent.

He continued. "Look at the wolves in the mountain and the fish in the sea. They kill, they eat, they reproduce, and they sleep. Do they think? Are they ever unhappy? Do they strive to submit themselves to God?"

A memory captured me.

"I was on a mission in Africa once," I said. "The termite mounds there are huge. I found them frightening at first, all created by unthinking insects living in their blind, restless communities. One evening, in the light of the sunset, the mounds they had created appeared to me as cathedrals."

"And?"

I paused to recollect. "And, I thought of how little I understood God's world and resolved to increase my efforts to be near Him."

He nodded, but again his face showed disappointment again, as if I had failed to understand something. We sat in silence for a time.

Finally, I spoke, for he seemed to me to be lost in an elementary error. "My son," I said, "we are indeed imperfect, but our minds and our spiritual strivings, these are gifts from God. They are the joys and, yes, sometimes burdens. He gave us these gifts to help us to understand and to praise Him, to do his works and to have dominion over His creation, to know Him better and to reach Him. Our activities have a higher aim than those of the animals. That wolf, that fish, those bees, they will not gain heaven. Their only perfection is right here and now.

He turned to me solemnly.

"No bees in heaven, Father?"

He bent forward with his arms across his knees and stared at the ground. A few ants wandered between the pebbles.

Then, he sat up and turned to me, staring into my eyes. "I think our minds and our strivings may be from something else."

I crossed myself three times. "Of course, they are," I said. "Or rather, they can be. There are so many wiles. That is why we are here, in this holy place. Please do not repeat that our activities are no different from those of the world."

"Father, do you know of Richard Strauss? When he was a child, he begged his parents to stop the music that constantly played in his mind. It tormented him. In time, he became a famous and wealthy composer. He was prolific and sensitive, but he also liked to drink beer and play cards with his friends. He wrote a number of operas—rich, decadent, and beautiful in their understanding of life.

"Then, he became, under duress, the minister of culture for Hitler's Nazis. He tried to help other musicians where he could.

"After the war, he underwent de-Nazification, quite pointlessly, as he was never really a Nazi. Late in life, he wrote four songs, his last songs. The most beautiful of them he set to the words of St. Paul, '. . . but the greatest of these is love.' Tell me, does this man's life make any sense at all? Wasn't he just a colorful piece of paper that blew about in the wind? And yet, he left us the *Four Last Songs*. All that came before was only restlessness. Perhaps those songs were, too."

I tried to explain to him that it was through Adam's fall and expulsion from Eden that we gained the knowledge of the world, but that in His mercy, God allows us to use that same knowledge to find our way back to him through Christ. I confess that, at one point, I realized I was repeating myself. I was not sure whether or not I was making sense with this line of argument. Was I?

He answered me like this. "The Garden of Eden is childhood, Father. Nothing more. When we are children, we are like the bee and the fish, perfectly following the plan that nature, or God, has set out for us. The curse of adulthood is the knowledge of good and evil, our knowledge of ourselves. And your theology cannot escape the fact that this too comes from God."

"It comes from disobedience to God," I said, rather loudly.

"But He built it into the plan, did He not? So it ultimately comes from Him."

His words were too clever. I rose to cast him out of our midst. Instead, I turned and embraced him.

I have not sent him away. He still tends the garden, and it is more beautiful and silent than ever.

We have not spoken in private since that day, six months ago. I confess that he seems to be, despite his heresy against dogma, a spiritually evolved person. He who seeks only the sound of the bee, the silence of the plants, and the movement of the wind. When he comes to Confession— always to me—he now says, "Thank you for your time with me, Father. Everything is fine now."

I have allowed him to remain. Have I done the right thing? He may be different among us, but there is also the possibility that he may be perfect in his service to the Almighty.

This man seems to me to understand something. Are we really not so different from the worldly? Are we in our ceaseless spiritual strivings also filling our minds with noise? Is a bee, in its perfect expression of the laws that govern it, perhaps a kind of angel?

Yours in Christ,

Father A—

John Grey

CEREMONIAL

Hills so high that
mind and breath separate.
The latter overcompensates
for rugged, rocky angles.
The former performs
for the bright, opal moon—
            A ceremony is about to commence—
If you haven't heard goats
bleating from deep in the valley,
you do not know what it is like
to be at elevations where there
are no goats—
            A ceremony
            could carry you out of midnight in a port city
            to the lush hills above the copper mines,
            where even the blackness
            is a thick, unalterable green—
In the distance,
thunder wipes lightning's slate clean.
Clouds hang off the horizon,
afraid to come nearer.
Other gods maintain this grid,
not the coquettish tramps of weather—
            A ceremony I was invited to watch
            ten years ago or so
awakens like white delphiniums,

a conveyor belt of bark huts,
sugar cane fields,
abandoned Christian churches
and old women with dark teeth
who chew the roots of the earth
solemnly, silently, spitting
the juice, the residue golden
in the cheerful rally of light—
In a cramped room,
I take the pilot's watch.
In the presence of dying,
centered by chaos of time,
the narrowness of space between
my gutting choices,
nothing on the dresser,
under the covers,
in the refrigerator,
that will let you live,
I bend over you.
Something I bought you dangles from your wrist,
red carnelian, the gem,
like a drop of blood
inside its plain glass limits,
the pleasure of an old wound
deliberating in mid air
but without a course of action—
A ceremony survives,
as accessible as air,
as primitive as the need

      to beg of your sunken eyes,
        as good, as heathen, as need's *odalisque* dancers—
You are dying of some kind of heresy
that would have me shiver to the poetry of grief,
limp as your hand.
The spaces between your exhalations
take up my pitiful case—
        But a ceremony unbraids the world.
        I am with the families now,
        close together in the galley
        but surely not enslaved,
        their voices chanting for oars,
        and the deep, black night,
        an incessant ocean,
        and the drums of a ritual march,
        stirring a togetherness
        out of the blinding patterns
        that just might secure you,
        the sound of mystery in your ears
        like splashing in a cave,
        a beautiful image of water
        rippling in your face—
I leave because I understand
your rescue can't include you,
burrow myself down by
boarded up waterfront bars,
a quiet quarry of humanity
where streets leave off at ocean's edge,
where a walk by myself
is a haphazard but truthful

understanding of your condition,
where old revelations
leave unseen moss on the stones,
and a holy grail,
stuck at the tip of my lips,
flutters slightly—
       The ceremony is unstoppable—
       the chief celebrant is an
       old bare-footed man
       in blue overalls,
       a white surplice
       draped over his shoulders,
       an affectionate parody
       of the parish priest,
       a robe I would cut up for wings,
       pin to your dishonest flesh—
You wonder how I can think
of ceremony,
but isn't it all
the clip-clop of my shoes,
slender cold wind,
the creak of boardwalk,
the buzzing of the lighthouse,
an apple tree with one blossom—
Your disease implies
a mouth this strange
and discordant religious music,
but the ceremony is all-inclusive—
       A handsome young man bears
       the *mamaloi* aloft,

a beautiful woman in crimson robe
and feathered headdress
on palms of memory,
shivers and shakes.
A history of solids
shimmy to liquid
in the naked light—
No blasphemy here
is not a thought
awash in mystical symbols,
or a tune.
A pagan gesture
to crush the serpents,
to unwind them like bandanas
with each note,
incites all reptiles to flee or perish.
I speak, I sing
to their primitive but wise geography where
Guinea is in the East, the sun sets
in the West, and yet, somehow, magically
rises again next morning in Guinea—
Unknown to you,
a ceremony ignores the turning
of the earth,
for explanation
finds you in some place old,
puts you somewhere new.

Pat Lipsky

An Interview with Pat Lipsky

Pat Lipsky has dedicated herself to painting for several decades. Lipsky graduated from Cornell University with a B.F.A. in 1963, following which she received an M.A. in painting at Hunter College. There, she studied with sculptor Tony Smith.

Lipsky's paintings have been reviewed by Ken Johnson (*The New York Times*), David Cohen (*The New York Sun*), Alicia Turner (*The Miami Herald*), Karen Wilkin (*Art in America*), and Alexi Worth (*The New Yorker*)—among others. Her paintings are in twenty-four public collections, including the Whitney, the Hirshhorn, and the San Francisco Museum of Modern Art, and she has had twenty-eight solo exhibits.

We caught up with Lipsky in her studio in downtown Manhattan. We talked ten floors above the Hudson River, seated in paint-splattered chairs, with her large simplified color paintings leaning against the walls.

We found Lipsky tall, quirky, and elegant, at ease in her signature t-shirt and jeans.

Lalitamba: What kind of images influenced you as a child?

Lipsky: As a child, I was interested in images that came from what I called *olden times*. I loved the rooms from Colonial America at the Brooklyn Museum. I thought that life had been better then. I liked the displays of people doing homey things, like churning butter or milking cows.

I would also look out the window into our backyard and imagine Indians running around out there.

I was interested in birds, too. Their different colors attracted me. I tried to memorize some of their names. Scarlet Tanager. Robin Red Breast. Blue Jay. Baltimore Oriole.

Then, one of my uncles returned from somewhere in South America—Venezuela, I think—after the war and brought back a tray made of butterfly wings. I was intrigued by their exotic patterns. Another uncle who'd survived the Battan Death March came to stay at our house. He'd done a painting of a red horse that really impressed me.

Lalitamba: Was there a moment or event that inspired you to paint?

Lipsky: I studied painting for a summer at the Brooklyn Museum Art School. I was sixteen. Rather than go to camp, I decided to take classes there every day. I was overwhelmed by the act of painting full time—like a real painter. It felt right to me, not like school, where art classes were punctuated by forty-minute bells.

The instructor, Moses Soyer, took me seriously. I set up a mirror in the class and did a self-portrait in a large studio at the school. This picture won first prize in the Scholastic Art Awards for high school seniors. Hallmark Cards acquired it, and it was also shown at what was then the New York Coliseum. My photo appeared in the *Brooklyn Eagle*. That was it.

Lalitamba: At what point did you realize that you were an artist, that this would be your life's work?

Lipsky: A short aside. I don't like the word artist. It sounds pretentious to me. Matisse considered himself a painter, and Picasso thought of himself as an artist. I prefer Matisse.

In graduate school, I still thought of myself as an art student. I studied with Tony Smith at Hunter College for four years, instead of the necessary one, just to keep the classes going. It was towards the end of this period that I started thinking of myself as a painter. I had gone to the studios at Hunter almost every day, as a painter would, and produced a body of work. I had my first solo show two years after graduating.

Lalitamba: Your paintings are often compared with and even titled for music. What kind of music would you say your paintings reflect? How is sound a part of your life?

Lipsky: Bach. I constantly listen to Bach and have for many years. I like other classical music, but Bach's work has actually influenced my painting, particularly his fugue format, his counterpoint, and his polyphony. Bach's music, like the *Well-Tempered Clavier*, the *Goldberg Variations*, and the *English Suites*, is abstract and not taken over by melody. The art critic Ken Johnson guessed that I was influenced by Bach without ever having talked with me about it. He mentioned a feeling of "Bach-like musicality" in a review he did of one of my shows in New York.

When I was a teenager, in the late fifties and early sixties, there was a lot of jazz around. I particularly liked Thelonoius Monk, who surprisingly turns out to have been influenced by Bach. Often, I went to the Blue Note, where he played.

Lipsky in the Studio

David Lipsky

The improvisational aspect and freedom of jazz appealed to me. I found it inherently American.

One of my favorite things is going to concerts, where I'm often soothed by music. Proust was right. Music provides "spiritual nourishment."

Lalitamba: You've also been translating Proust. How does your work with Proust's writing emanate from your life as a painter?

Lipsky: Good question, although I'm not sure it does. It may be the other way around. I did a painting called *Proust's Sea*, which came out of my translation work, because the author mentions the sea so much. Also, the triptych *Oceans* came directly out of a passage I was translating, in which the writer describes a Nereid frolicking in the ocean. I think I'm influenced by the poetry in Proust's writing. My father was an amateur poet, and he read poems to me when I was a young child. Somehow, among other things, the language of Proust evokes that memory. His work is also very visual. He writes scenes and describes things that one can see.

Lalitamba: What is there about Proust's writing that calls you to translate his words?

Lipsky: I have been captivated by *À la recherche du temps perdu*. During some crisis or other over the last forty years, I've managed to read all six volumes three times.

I first became acquainted with *Swann's Way*, when I was nineteen.

In 2004, I got the idea to look at the original French of Book II, *In the Shadow of Young Girls in Flower*, which, for personal reasons had taken on special meaning for me. That was surprising. The English translation seemed unnecessarily different from the French. Words were added and phrases altered. To my mind, the translation wasn't entirely honest. I thought perhaps it could be done better? For a work that has changed every part of my life, that has become a filter for my thoughts and opinions, a prism through which to view my existence, it seemed a worthwhile attempt.

Lalitamba: Christianity seems to appear frequently in your work—*Episcopalian Pandemonium* is the title of one of your early paintings and, more recently, there is the series *Les Vitraux*. What's the connection?

Lipsky: The title *Episcopalian Pandemonium* and my series *Les Vitraux* have nothing to do with Christianity. *Episcopalian Pandemonium* is a title that I lifted directly from a line in a play by T. S. Eliot. The phrase represented the over one hundred colored squares that made up my ten foot painting. Maybe my father's thought would have been better. "To me, it looks like dancing."

My series, *Les Vitraux*, "stained glass windows" in French, has to do with color. I was strongly influenced by the 12th and 13th century windows in French cathedrals like Chartres, Bourges, Le Man, Troyes and others that I visited between 2000 and 2004. I was impressed by the *fauve* colors that these glassmakers invented. I thought that they were the true Fauve painters. I decided to do a series entirely different from my other work, based on these charming medieval images that were clearly inspired by religion. I learned a lot about the *Bible*, both the Old and New Testaments, from this project. Almost all of the ancient windows, with the exceptions of those of the Zodiac and Charlemagne at Chartres, are derived from religious topics.

Lalitamba: What role does God, the transcendent, or the sublime play in your art?

Lipsky: God plays no part. I don't think in those terms, though it is possible that I am going for a transcendent effect in my painting. I think of getting an image that resonates, that has some magic to it, that creates an aura. It's that "there it is" feeling. Really, it's not something you can put into words. If you could, you wouldn't have to paint it.

Lalitamba: What is your personal theory on art?

Lipsky: I don't have a personal theory of art. With me, it's all practice, intuitive. I remember hearing about Mondrian, that he would ask anyone who walked into his studio if a line or division was in the right place, or whether it should be moved. For me, painting is experimental. Trial and error. I keep trying things until something finally looks right.

Lalitamba: What makes good art?

Lipsky: What makes good art? That's a tough question, I don't know if I can answer that. Maybe some of the ingredients are cohesiveness and feeling. It's about creating something that adds to the language of art, while maintaining the standards of the past. This includes the painter's ability to successfully resolve problems she or he has set out in the work's structure.

Lalitamba: What is the purpose of art?

Lipsky: "The purpose of art" is a long and contentious question. So many different painters and writers have weighed in on it. I like what Proust wrote about artistic expression in *À la recherche du temps perdu*:

> "By art alone we are able to get outside ourselves, to know what another sees of this universe which for him is not ours, the landscapes of which would remain as unknown to us as those of the moon. Thanks to art, instead of seeing one world—our own—we see it multiplied. As many original artists as there are, so many worlds are at our disposal, differing more widely from each other than those which roll around the infinite and which, whether their name be Rembrandt or Vermeer, send us their unique rays many centuries after the hearth from which they emanate is extinguished."

Finally, there is aesthetic experience. For the time that you are looking at the work, or listening to it, you are connecting with the creator in a disinterested way. Nothing

Lipsky on Madison Avenue

David Lipsky

in your life is going to change, but you are allowing yourself to be moved. You are exercising your unique humanness.

Lalitamba: Is there an underlying philosophy to the way you live your life?

Lipsky: Probably there is. I believe in art, in making art. That and being a mother have been the focus of my life.

Jessica Chen

PROBABLE IMPOSSIBILITY

It had been a month, since the last time Yu-Ling had talked to her mother.

Walking along the South Bank in London, Yu-Ling wondered why she had not phoned her. After pondering this for a while, she put it in the back of her mind.

Yu-Ling looked across the River Thames at the pointed dome of St. Paul's Cathedral. It was huge. The golden cross atop the cathedral glittered under the sunlight.

For a few seconds, she did not move.

She stood and stared at the shiny cross. She was not a Christian. No, and her mother wasn't either. Her mother was a devoted Buddhist, though that did not make her life any better.

Yu-Ling remembered how she'd been crazy about Nietzsche and all those atheist ideas, back in high school. Stupid.

As she'd reached her legal age, Yu-Ling had come to this conclusion. Atheism was a religion in its own way, same as Communism. People were always trying to make up something to believe in, so that they could continue their miserable lives. Thus, she had declared herself as an agnostic. After all, Yu-Ling did not want to have anything to do with religion.

Nevertheless, for some strange reason, the cross atop St. Paul's looked beautiful.

It was an unusually sunny day for London in early June. The sun was burning hot. Yu-Ling felt herself starting to sweat.

When the heat became unbearable, Yu-Ling looked for a cooler place. She entered the Tate Modern Museum. She was still wondering what to do with the two-month old child in her womb.

* * *

As a person, Rodin really sucks, Yu-Ling thought. She stood in front of *The Kiss* with a blank face. She admired Auguste Rodin as an artist, like she admired Pablo Picasso. They were both acclaimed male artists who stole inspirations from women and treated the opposite sex like inflatable dolls. Such jerks.

Tourists swarmed in like bees. Yu-Ling took a step closer to look at the marble statue. The naked, lifeless couple fervently kissed one another.

Poor Paolo. Yu-Ling thought. *If he knew that Francesca's husband would come in to kill them both, he would probably remove his hand from her hip as quickly as possible and help get her dressed.* Yu-Ling could not help but smile.

She heard a female voice behind her say, "So romantic. They must be passionately in love."

It reminded her that she had passionately dumped a man after being passionately dumped by a woman, all in the past three months.

The air inside the museum was cool. Yu-Ling stopped sweating. She gazed at Francesca's stone arm around Paolo's bending neck. For a moment, she wished that she could be like Dante, so bitchy to everyone in his writing.

But she was not Dante. Besides, she did not love the woman who had dumped her enough to hate her or to write a book. She'd slept with that woman, but only because she did not want to sleep alone. The fatal mistake she'd made was getting drunk after being dumped, after which she'd left the bar and picked up a random guy off the street, flinging herself onto him like an Asian hooker.

Yu-Ling had always imagined that she would be the one to dump the woman.

The cool air breezed over her bare skin. She felt chilly.

She began to roam around the museum. A group of teenagers passed by. She recognized them as Americans by their familiar accent.

She could not figure out why, after ten years of studying in the United States, she had not gone back home. Instead, she had gone to England and screwed up her life. *There must be something wrong with me*, she thought. Indeed, didn't she miss home all the time?

"Why? Baby, don't cry, don't cry. Everything will be alright."

The night she got dumped and drunk, she'd forced a random guy to do her in a dark alley. He had whispered those words to her. It was a disgusting place to have sex—even for a dog. That guy was perhaps worse than a dog. He kept talking and talking and pressing his fat lips against her eyelids. His month stank. His lips felt like a pair of worms. Nevertheless, what Yu-Ling regretted most was waking up the next morning in the hotel room with him. The man snoring beside her appeared to be a young Caucasian male.

She blushed, ashamed.

Yu-Ling never had ceased to think of herself as a traitor, even after the relationship ended. She had become one of those Asian girls who slept with white men.

She stopped in front of a life-sized portrait of a naked, middle-aged white man. He seemed to be a sloppy homeless man. His hair was uncombed and his chest, sunken. Yu-Ling took a long look at his open crotch. *Joe Gould should sue Alice Neel because she not only tripled his penis but also drew it too small. She made him look like an impotent sex offender*, she thought.

Yu-Ling raised her eyebrows. She noticed a little blond boy standing next to her. He was about five. The boy was squinting at the painting.

"Dad, how come he has three? Girls won't—"

Yu-Ling walked away to avoid hearing the rest. *British sex education rocks.* She sighed when she saw that there were at least five elementary-age kids in the room with her. *What kind of parents would bring their children to the Tate Modern, anyway? Is that any sort of parental guidance?* She wanted to find their parents, yell at them, and smack their pointed noses. Instead, she left the gallery without saying a word.

Her stomach began to growl. She needed to eat.

* * *

The cream of mushroom soup was warm on her throat. Yu-Ling lowered her shoulders and leaned back into the couch.

It was noon. Groups of tourists were strolling in and out of the museum. Yu-Ling was glad that she'd arrived early.

She preferred this view from the café on the second floor to the one from the restaurant on the seventh. She liked to watch people.

"Hiya, this is Chris. Right...Christopher Huffman. I need to talk with you..."

A man with a suitcase rushed out of the café while talking on his mobile phone. He moved so fast that Yu-Ling could not see his face. Only the back of a bald head was exposed. She felt sorry for this Christopher Huffman, a mundane Englishman.

She turned to watch him through the glass wall behind her. He had a pale face and protruding eyes. He was still talking on his mobile. He looked like a frog, croaking and jumping.

He reminded Yu-Ling of her father.

Yu-Ling was glad that the man she had slept with for the past three months had nothing in common with her father. The man she had slept with was an American tourist. He had just graduated from college and was taking a year off to explore Europe. He was five years younger than she was. Immature. Shallow. Idealist. She would rather die than marry him. There was no way she would start a family with him. Sex only.

She turned back and grabbed her sandwich from the porcelain plate. Before she could swallow the first bite of goaty-smelling mozzarella, a sour taste filled her mouth. She grabbed her bag and ran to the restroom.

Pathetic, she thought. Her life was a failure. Her breakfast dropped into the toilet bowl. A few splashes of water hit her face.

Yu-Ling flushed the toilet. Her legs felt heavy, as she made her way to the sink.

The Asian woman she saw in the mirror looked tired. Her thick make-up was smeared. There was vomit stuck in her hair. Smelly. Disgusting. Yu-Ling could not understand why this woman had let herself end up like this.

Why?

Two moist black eyes glared back at her.

How?

She wanted to punch the mirror.

What should she do with the child?

Yu-Ling bit at her lower lip with a feeling that she did not know how to express. Her chest felt hollow. She turned the water on. Her head sank into the sink. She closed her eyes. As the cold water ran over her face, she could taste the dissolving make-up. Somehow, she felt relieved.

* * *

Yu-Ling stayed in her apartment for the rest of the day. She lay on the sofa and watched TV, all afternoon and into the evening. When she saw something hilarious—especially super fake TV shows like *Britain's Got Talent*—she couldn't help but giggle.

The woman she used to sleep with liked those shows. Yu-Ling was glad that they had parted.

She did not go upstairs to her studio that day. Yeah, she had a painting to finish. So what.

The *masala* she bought from the local grocery was edible, as usual. After finishing her microwave dinner, she left the plates in the kitchen sink and went to bed. She changed into her pajamas and started to think about Hamlet. Of course, he was a coward. Or was he? Yu-Ling did not know enough about Shakespeare to answer that question.

The woman she used to sleep with loved Shakespeare. She was an actress.

Yu-Ling preferred Horatio to Hamlet. *But Horatio lost his country in the end. He became homeless and got that damned responsibility from Hamlet to tell the story.*

Yu-Ling pressed her face against the pillow. She wondered what the Buddha would say about the child.

He would probably be a pro-choice pro-lifer, who thinks killing is bad and also believes that the mother has a right to choose.

Yu-Ling was not a Buddhist. Her mother was. When Yu-Ling was little, her mother used to light incense. Yu-Ling still liked that smell. It soothed her. She remembered doing Buddhist practice with her mother. Most of the time her father had not been at home.

Yu-Ling would not forget how hard she had cried, begging her father not to leave, and how easily he had rejected her.

When she grew older, Yu-Ling realized that, among all the religions, she hated Buddhism the most. It had made her mother accept the unfairness of life.

In Yu-Ling's opinion, her mother did not act like a normal human being. Whenever Yu-Ling did something wrong, her mother did not scream or slap her. She would give Yu-Ling that nasty, peaceful smile and tell her not to do the same next time.

"What is done is done. Don't get upset, Yu-Ling. It's not your fault."

No, it's entirely my fault. Yu-Ling clutched at the pillow. *It's because of me that you became infertile and Dad knew that he would never get a boy.*

She wanted to scream and to wake the neighbors up. Her mother was always patient with Yu-Ling's tears. When she cried, her mother would hold her and pat her head. She would help Yu-Ling to hide her ugly face. She was too nice.

Yu-Ling pressed her lips tight, but her teeth trembled. She could still remember from childhood how warm her mother's breast had been.

Every time her mother held her now, she could hear her heart beating.

But Yu-Ling guessed that her mother's kindness was an excuse to mess up every thing. How could it not be?

Her mother never punished her, therefore, it seemed to Yu-Ling that she didn't care about her as a daughter.

Then, who cared about her as a daughter?

Her father had turned away from her, because of her sex. So, she grew up wanting to be like a boy. She wanted to be tough. She wanted to be independent.

She'd gone to the United States at age fourteen and lived by herself, but no matter how hard she tried, she could never be a boy, could not pass on their lineage. Her existence was a joke. She knew in her heart that she was a failure.

After studying for ten years in the United States, she'd grown tired of that country. Then, she'd moved to England.

Why hadn't she gone home?

Why? Her father despised her. When he heard that she was going to attend art school, however, he paid the tuition. Five thousands bucks was what she received from him monthly. The money was trivial to him. Her half-brother was going to Harvard this year.

She knew she was an ungrateful child. What did she want, exactly? She did not know.

At one point, she had thought that she would not ever dump the woman, but the woman had dumped her. She was tired. She wanted to sleep. And now, there was a two-month-old child in her womb. If her existence was a pathetic joke, this life surely meant suffering.

Yu-Ling fell asleep around 2:00 a.m.

She did not wake up until noon.

* * *

The Thames looks dirty. Compared to this, the Seine is much cleaner, but Paris is an awful city where dogs crap on every street. Awful. Yu-Ling stood on the South Bank. Besides staring at the muddy water, she had nothing to do.

That afternoon, she had gone to see *Les Misérables*.

Because she had nothing particular to do, she'd gone to the West End to have lunch in Chinatown and watch a musical. The Wednesday matinee attracted fewer tourists. The theater felt cozy.

Yu-Ling had never really liked musicals.

The woman she used to sleep with worked in musical theater, so she had tried her best to like them. It just didn't work out.

There were so many cheesy musicals that irritated her. Most of the time, she left at the intermission.

Les Miz, however, was different. At least the plot did not suck. Yu-Ling gazed at her twisted reflection on the Thames. *If Javert had been English, would he have jumped off the bridge?*

It seemed to her that drowning had been romanticized. Ophelia had drowned herself, and Sir John Everrett Millais made a beautiful painting for her, which was now in the Tate British. Virginia Woolf, her all time favorite writer, had drowned herself. *Did Woolf realize that she would become an ugly corpse, when she jumped into the water?*

Reflected in the water, her face looked puzzled.

She did not want to be ugly. Neither did she want to be in pain. Her life was not all that miserable compared to so many people in Africa. She should be grateful. Her father was rich. She would not be one of those starving artists. Her paintings sold alright. Most critics said nice things about her work. She had everything she needed to maintain a decent lifestyle. But she also had a child. A child—A two-month-old child in her womb. What should she do with the child?

She was sure that she would not be a good mother. She was not even a good daughter. She wished she could give this child everything she had, but there was something she did not know how to give.

Yu-Ling bent down to take a closer look at the filthy water.

The weather was not good. Gray clouds floated over the river. She wanted to see through the water. She wanted an answer to her question.

What would her mother say?

Perhaps her mother would get mad this time, or perhaps she would say, "Come. I'll take care of the child."

Yu-Ling did not want her mother to take care of the child. She did not want this child to grow up as she had. This child deserved something better.

Besides, this child would be a mutt. How would other people treat him or her? How much suffering would her child need to endure during his or her life? *Life really is not fair*.

She was so tired. She wanted to feel fresh water on her skin. What her mother would say did not matter anymore.

"Hey, be careful, young lady. You almost fell," a rusty male voice shouted behind her.

Yu-Ling looked up. A man who looked exactly like Joe Gould in that painting stared back at her. He was clothed, though.

"Are you okay? Got some problems? Maybe we can talk," the stranger said. His bushy black eyebrows frowned. He seemed to be worried about her.

Realizing what she might have done if this man had not appeared, Yu-Ling stood there with her mouth opened. Her legs trembled.

"Do you speak English? Can you understand me?" the man asked.

He was probably homeless.

Yu-Ling tried to murmur something, but she could not. She burst into tears. Those salty, hot tears smeared her mascara. She could no longer be cold. What might she have done? What might she have done to her baby? Her breath choked. Her sight blurred, so that she could not see the homeless man.

She was glad that there seemed to be somebody who cared about her.

* * *

Yu-Ling took the tube back to her apartment. *What's done is done.* She looked at her reflection in the tube window. The long, narrow tunnel appeared to start nowhere and head nowhere. It seemed to crack as the tube wheels hit against the track. Indeed, the wheels were loud.

The train traveled with great noise in the darkness.

When the light came back again, Yu-Ling exited at South Kensington. She walked back to her apartment and washed the dirty plates she had left in the kitchen sink. When she had finished with the cleaning, she sat down on her bed. She picked up the phone. Without hesitation, she dialed her mother.

Drew Roberts

THE HERE THE GONE BRINGS

I welcome what others shun and shun what others welcome.
I study what others ignore and ignore what others study.
I avoid what others strive for
and strive for what others avoid.
I know the extent to which we are different,
because I know the extent to which
      we are the same.
It is impossible for two things to be the same.
It is also impossible for two things to be dissimilar.
It is impossible to love anything without loving everything.
My body knows everything about everything.
The only reason my mind does not is that my mind does not
speak the same
      language as my body...yet.

I cherish misery in the moments I am not miserable.
The goal, of course, is to cherish it always.
If I go too long without misery, my body will feel it, the
aching lack of it, and find a
      way to bring it back.
In this I am no different than anyone.
I am terrified
and relieved to be.

Denise Shekerjian

FOR THE BIRDS

I was not always a bird person. I don't recall any memorable birds with regard to my early years. Later, my city years were marked mostly by pigeons. On fortunate weekends, there were gulls and sandpipers on the Jersey Shore. This was what I knew about birds. Such was the happy sum of my bird experience, until a move north some decades ago changed everything.

The house where my husband and I settled and raised our boys sits in a protected cove. It is ringed by wetlands and plenty of New England forest. Birds delight in the red cedars that rim the yard. The blue-gray juniper berries attract them, but once in the neighborhood, they soon find my bird feeder, which I keep well-filled with quality seed.

The feeder was built by my father some ten years ago, when he was in his vigorous late-seventies. The project had been begun and abandoned by one of my sons. When my father visited, restless for something to do that would be both helpful and satisfying, he embraced the challenge with gusto.

My father had grown from a city boy into a suburban man. If birds had entered the equation for him before this, he never mentioned it. Indeed, I would have described my father as a reliable physician of the old school variety. He was good with his hands, and handy around the house. This included my house.

The plans for the project included a picture which promised a beautiful feeder—a Victorian cottage pavilion that was small, white, tasteful, and square. It was fetching for its seeming simplicity, though intricate in its construction.

My father made a serious study of the plans at the kitchen table. He composed a list of what he needed and descended the stairs to the basement, to survey the jumble of my workroom in search of his supplies.

Gingerly, my father sifted through the disarray. He collected what he needed, as if he were gathering eggs from a hen house. Some items were missing. The little dowels for the porch, for example, and the trim for the railings. Finally, he boxed up whatever he could find and packed it into his suitcase.

"I'll see what I can do," he promised.

I had no doubt that he would return with a Victorian cottage bird feeder.

It is not irrelevant to mention that my father was a man of science and that my mother had an active spiritual life. These two things do not belong in the same sentence, let alone the same household. The result was an eclectic conversation that ranged over fifty-four years of a loving marriage. But that was them.

From a child's point of view, their different ways of sizing up the world presented practical questions. When something ached, did I go to my father for a balm or my mother for a laying-on of hands?

Of course, my mother might just as easily recommend a redirection of energies, a meditation, or a dream analysis. Once, we walked barefooted on a bed of fire together. The exercise was overseen by a pair of strong-willed, dark, and wild Russian women whom my exuberant mother had befriended.

In the push-pull of debate in my household as to how healing happens, it seemed that my parents would never agree. The most acute area of division was over the matter of what happened when healing failed. What happened when the ailing person died?

They agreed, at least, on this much. Death should be kind.

But after that, what, if anything, came next?

She'd paint a picture of the bright promise of an afterlife, her voice light and assured, as she stirred a pot on the stove. From time to time, she pointed the spoon in my father's direction for emphasis.

Sitting at the kitchen table, he'd look up from his newspaper and shake his head in amusement. "But darling, how do you know for sure?"

In some homes, the church has the last say on the question of life after death. The church that stood at the center of my extended family had clear views on the matter.

At the heart of the Armenian Orthodox culture from which I hail, it stood—a soaring edifice, gold-peaked, filled with incense, glittering with brass and silver, and lit by candles deep in its dusky reaches. The music that filled the dome was especially compelling. Our minor tones and musical phrases never quite resolved as the ear expected them to.

My immigrant grandfather had had a heavy hand in the building of this structure. The church was the beginning and the end of who we were, what we believed. It was the place we sent our children for *Bible* lessons, kissed our aunties' powdered cheeks, bought baked goods, and invited the priest for the Sunday meal. It was the place we hoped that our children would meet their spouses.

I was required to go, but I had already acquired the basic teachings from my grandmother. She had seen to these matters at an early age. Life everlasting figured prominently in the lessons, a lack of specificity notwithstanding.

I'm quite sure that my mother received the same lessons. Still, she grew into a modern woman. She was stylish and lively, with shiny dark hair and red lipstick. She wore circle skirts and Bermuda shorts. Along the way, her spiritual views shifted decidedly towards the East. She cultivated her new spiritual interests with vigor. She believed in *karma* and the afterlife, which she presumed was better than everyday life. She maintained that what came to a person is what a person earned, that every challenge is a lesson, that angels guide us, and that the long-dead advise us. She trusted the old aunties who poured thick coffee and read the muddy grinds. She knew and consulted a wide range of psychics. She looked them up all over the world. She did healing work, read auras, went to lectures and workshops, hosted book discussions, invited spoon benders to dinner, championed certain physicists, was at the forefront of the hospice movement, trusted her instincts, and thought that death should be peaceful. She wasn't afraid of death. Not at all. And if we needed that reminder, she'd be happy to supply it.

My father felt differently. He took little comfort in her explanations and assurances. Spoon benders, mind readers, fortune tellers—these things were rubbish. They were "for the birds," as he put it. He was on staff at four hospitals, had a private practice, and freelanced for the coroner's office. He was a surgeon, and he knew death to be the cold emptiness of a stiff body, the skin gone ashy, the chest thick and still. That was death, he said. No one home. There wasn't much to recommend it. He saw nothing romantic about it.

Besides, he loved his life. He was the kind of man who ate with relish, told jokes, charmed the ladies, and adored my mother. Breakfast was his favorite meal, and he rose each day in anticipation of it. He sang with his head thrown back. He cried at something beautiful. He played the violin and enjoyed his Scotch, before he lost the taste for it. The idea of death was damned inconvenient.

"The long habit of living indisposeth us for dying," said Sir Thomas Browne. My father certainly agreed. He saw no reason for my mother's joyous anticipation of her passing.

Still, she held to her views.

"I want to go home," my mother would say, breezily, self-assured.

He'd look up from his toast, his brows knit with momentary confusion. "But sweetheart, aren't we home?"

* * *

When he first mounted the bird feeder on a squirrel-proof pole, it sparkled like a little white palace. The peaked roof shaded the base, around which ran a miniature fence made of decorative railings. The doll house shingles on the roof were his idea, as was the copper piping along the seams.

From the outset, he fretted over its durability. He worried about the roof. He was concerned about moisture, about shingles lifting in the storms and being carried away by the strong gusts off the lake. He sealed it well, reflected on the bitter temperatures of a Vermont winter, and sealed it again. When at last it was put to service, he was pleased to see it in place, and happy that from the first hour, his well-constructed feeder did a healthy business.

There were a number of birds that visited, and though my father moved on to other tasks, I kept binoculars and guide books within easy reach. With my sons, I had already catalogued the butterflies, mosses, and mushrooms of our woods and fields. My ambition now was simply to learn about them.

I made a study of things. Birds come to my feeder year-round in their shifting migrations, and on a given day, this is what I might observe:

> three or four species
> three or four birds of each kind
> maybe a woodpecker once in a while
> but never an owl, not so close to home

If I chatted with my father about the birds I had seen, he asked only, "How's the feeder?" What he meant was, *Is it holding up? Did the shingles stay put?*

* * *

About seven years into the life of the feeder, my father's health took a turn for the worse. Everyone was running amuck in the harsh realities that came to light. The old order was gone, and the new one required an adjustment to all things financial, filial, and faithful. Some members of the family were in hell. Others clutched two-fisted to crazy dreams. A few hid under the covers, and a few more stomped around trying to fix things. I entered all of these camps and emerged pretty weary for it. In the meantime, my father grew frail. We moved him to the assisted living facility of his residence.

It seemed clear that this would be the last move for him, and I visited often. I took early flights and returned late, sometimes on the same day. Once back in Vermont, I resumed my day-to-day duties in the household.

One morning, just at dawn, something strange appeared at the feeder. I put my mug down and, like some cartoon character, rubbed my eyes with my fists. What was this? Pink. Green. Blue. Yellow. Stripes. Dots. I reached for the binoculars and brought it into sharper focus. It was as if a stray, a bohemian little thing, a candy-colored guest, had arrived at a dinner far more subdued than it was.

I flipped through the guidebooks. Soon, I found myself in the pages reserved for the tropics. This couldn't be a tropical bird, though. Winter was coming, and if it were tropical, it would die.

I didn't want any more death. I'd had enough with the smaller deaths of distant relations, the big deaths of my dreams, and of course the inevitable mortal death of my father whose last strength was reserved to sip a bit of water. What would I want with more death out my very window?

I searched the books, looking for a Northern version of a parrot. I turned the pages in a fever. This, however, was a parakeet. There was no question about it, and the bird lived at the feeder my father had built.

Throughout the next days and weeks, I traveled to see my father.

While at home, I sat at the dining room table. I worked to piece together the new order that would define my mother's remaining days.

So, I enjoyed that little bird. It was a budgie. I came to know its habits and personality.

At first, it was cautious. It kept itself tucked deeply into the branches. I had to look hard to spot its ridiculous colors.

In time, shyly, tentatively, it swept in to the feeder. It would snatch the smallest of the seeds, for its mouth was tiny, and fly back to the safety of the branches.

At first, it fed alone, which made me sad. As the weeks progressed, however, I noticed that the chickadees took it in. Increasingly, its confidence grew. If I was having a lousy time of it in the dining room, I had only to look to its example to feel better.

With a lack of artifice, it had embraced its strange new world and made a decent life for itself. It even began to linger at the feeder. Once, it mustered the boldness to take on a blue jay, which had tried to commandeer the seed. The effort failed, of course, for the blue jay was three times its size, but I admired the spunk.

"Cheeky little thing," I mused aloud—and the name stuck.

But for all of Cheeky's boldness, the leaves on the trees turned colors. Some were fallen. Halloween was nearing and the weather was always iffy by then. Winter would soon arrive.

The chickadees wintered here, but would a tropical bird survive? We made some calls to the local experts. The consensus was united. Without an intervention of some kind, it would die before the year was out.

Winter here looks like this: the windows closed and locked, the firewood stacked, the heat turned on, the cold rain first, then frost on the windows, now sleet, now slush, now snow, an hour of shoveling just to clear access to the house, and in the harshest years, an impenetrable overcoat of ice on everything, tree branches snapping, no power, no phones, and snowmelt from the roof for water.

What would the bird do when the wind howled, and the snow fell? This question provoked a moral debate in our household. Was it right to capture it and see to its confinement, if such heroics were meant to save its life?

It had a full life, best as I could tell, with the wide open sky above, and the lake, marsh, and forests below. It had the companionship of the amiable chickadees. It was, in my view, that most desirous of things. Free. Was captivity a better choice than certain death? I had my doubts. Still, there was a chill in the air. The bird's feathers were fluffed up now at the feeder in an effort to stay warm.

When we took a family vote, I sided with life. Besides, I told myself, there was no guarantee that we could capture it. That made the question academic.

But one son took on the challenge and succeeded— bare-handed, third try, at the feeder.

It was a decent cage. We had seen to that. It had little bells and swings, and a mirror to trick the bird into thinking that it was not alone.

Still, the cage bothered me. In fact, it bothered everyone, and so we converted a bathroom into an aviary. We used branches and hung thistle seed, and when it was clear that Cheeky preferred a high perch, my son put a lump of wet sod over a light fixture for the bird's enjoyment. None of it worked. The confinement seemed wrong. As if in proof, the bird just sat at the window, stared at the chickadees, and didn't sing anymore. It needed a better home.

It took some days, but I found one, in the lobby of a veterinarian's office. The doctor was "a bird man," people said. I was very happy to hear it. This was a much bigger cage, with heat lamps and tropical-printed fabrics as a backdrop. Best of all, it came with the companionship of a distinguished gray parrot named Winston.

Our bird was so happy that it sang all day, the ladies of the office reported. This news was particularly well-timed. Sleet had iced the world the night before.

So, the bird lived, as my father died. I was glad for the bird, but it was my father's decline that pressed.

* * *

Thanksgiving came and went, and Christmas was soon upon us. I continued my migrations to and from my family of origin. I spent most of the time at my father's side.

The days were an ordered progression of hours. My mother was his constant companion. My siblings visited often.

Whenever anyone he loved walked in, his face would burst into a thousand smiles. His eyes were like exploding stars.

The nights, however, were something else. I recall them as a long stretch of hard hours that were fraught with a thousand questions. What does a death do but sharpen life? There is a looking back, a long view of the journey, which never matches what we'd expected at the start of the day. What does death do but clarify?

A man lay dying. He was my father, and this fact was as unsentimental as any I could imagine. What mattered now was how to ease his remaining time, to soothe his breath, to calm his brow, and to wait for the sun to rise.

His eyes were open, but opaque and unseeing. He would talk to someone or something that those of us at his bedside could not perceive.

"Open," he kept insisting, plucking at the gown that covered his chest. We adjusted his clothing, but this did not calm him. "Show me how," he repeated over and over. And by the morning, just shy of his 88th birthday and the day before Christmas, he was gone.

The call came early. I had flown back late that night.

When I received the news, I wrapped myself in a robe, crept downstairs, and started the coffee brewing. I stared numbly out the window, while the coffee perked. It was a solitary and frigid landscape. Not a breath was stirring in the air. The cove had iced over, but the ferry still ran in open water. Except for its silent crossing, nothing moved. The prayer flags were quiet. The bird feeder was covered with a thick layer of snow. It pained me to see how, despite my various ministrations, the small cottage had fallen into disrepair, just

as my father had feared it would. Bits of dowels were missing,
as were half the shingles. A piece of the porch had rotted clear
through. Empty of seed, it was empty of birds. It seemed that
on all battlefronts, I had lost.

And then something weird happened.

the cardinals were first
not three or four but at least eight or nine
hanging like holiday ornaments in the cedars
then the robins
in December
a flock of them a robust gang of 14? 20?
then nuthatches
the crested waxwings
chickadees
house wrens
so many blue jays
and not one but three species of woodpeckers
the red bellied
the yellow bellied
and the pileated
the last a very large bird
there were crows
out-numbered
sparrows
dozens of them
the poor plain cow birds
underdressed for this party
and the goldfinch
an unmistakable bird in the winter?

the orange flash of a scarlet tanager
a bird I rarely see
this was ridiculous, astonishing
more robins now
battalions of them at the front of the house
the house is surrounded
the great blue heron flies by
a single owl is deep in the cedar branches

"What's with the birds?" my children asked.

swallows
swifts
warblers
finches
red-winged black birds
the air vibrating with so much activity
hollow bones riding the wind
little tiny hearts beating in feathered breasts

"Strange," my husband said, a man of science.
Two hours later, they were gone.
A year later, I still think about those birds.
As my father's child, I looked for reasonable answers.
As my mother's child, I had to ask, *Was this then the work of my father?* Could it be that the newly deceased are afforded the chance to bestow a kind of last gift to the living world, a postcard from the new frontier, a poetic footnote to the old? It was a tender idea, bittersweet from every angle of consideration.

In my father's case, I felt as if he had used it this last chance as the opportunity to tidy up and leave the place in good order after the messy passions of life.

I pictured him on his journey, his back to us as he left the mortal realm. I imagined how he turned, at the last instant, to speak over his shoulder, and on his breath came the birds. "Never mind all that crap that passes for life. It doesn't matter, honey. It's all good in the end."

I know this much. There were an awful lot of birds out the window, a view that only a moment before had been a frigid still-life landscape. With the air quivering and the trees decked out in color, I felt as if, in the flutter of those wings, the old was swept away and new life breathed.

The dimensions of death surprise me. There is a business side: the arrangements, the responsibilities, the will, the bill. There is a practical side: the readjustments, the realignments, the realities. And there is, of course, an emotional side—our faces puffy and wrecked with grief.

But until the birds arrived, I hadn't known about a tender side, with the last word going to the dead. Not even my mother had predicted this.

Meanwhile, a year has passed. I am still a student, and I collect facts where I can find them.

I am also a pilgrim now, with my faith set firmly in the grace and wisdom of the natural world. Does it surprise anyone that I pay particular attention to the birds?

My guess is that my dad and I are both confirmed bird people, now.

As for the feeder, it's still there.

Simon Perchik

UNTITLED POEM

You were buried in the afternoon
and yet the moon was lost
on its way to the sea—what's left

is each night step by step
swallowing the light it needs
to swell—your grave will brighten soon

grow branches, more names, splash
—here is that sea and from the night
a grief-stone no bigger than a star

will fall into the waves rising as sunlight
made from sunlight and whitecaps
that pass by as spray that is not shoreline

right and left, smelling from salt
and your shadow with nothing left to let go
shimmering as if something happened.

Stuart Friebert

JOB'S TEARS

What some south of here call spiderwort,
its flowers in the early afternoon turn
into teardrops. Once, coming through your

garden with a tired step, I found you crying
again, which you denied. "I'm just in clouds
is all, trying to see through to a safe landing."

I tried to say nothing at all, maintain a manly
face as always. You'd been affected much more
than I by what we'd been through. What a strange

thing the habit of dying is. "A child may die
without any intention of doing so," you said,
swaying from side to side. Like a plow cutting

the earth, I'd planted my anger as if there were
no other remedy, while you resisted temptation
to think nothing had happened yet. The truth was only

a matter of imagining. You seemed relieved
when I went away, and prayed as if from some
distant memory, put the bible open on

your lap, swung your body around, dove into
the pond. Your breath bubbled up from below.

Betty Gabrielli

LOVE SONG

You offer me
longevity,
the miles
I'm wanting.

You're protected:
plates of galvanized
steel,
coatings of zinc.

I guard against rattles:
body fused
by a thousand welds,
yards of seal.

We're powered by an
engine that's satisfied
400 billion.

Inside are
big readable
instruments
we delight to use

and a level
of workmanship
few dream
of finding.

Actual mileage
may differ
according to distance
or hazards of the road.

Rick Kempa

INTO THE CALM

One person. Only one amongst all whom I've encountered in four decades of hiking the canyon country exists in memory as he who was at home there. In his eyes, in his bearing, in the presence he exuded, it was clearly written. He had been somewhere that mere distance could not measure.

I met him in the middle of a switchback-ridden slope, on a rim-to-river trail. From above, I watched him approach. He was a lean figure. He bent slightly forward against the steep grade. His long legs took every obstacle in stride. He seemed to be gliding rather than climbing.

This fluidity was marvelous to behold, for at the outset of my own hike, I was jump-starting and stalling my way downhill. I was feeling for the first rhythms.

As he neared, I called out in greeting.

He glanced up from a patch of earth on which he had been focused, and gave me a small nod. His face was neither open nor closed. He took me in, as one would take in a large boulder that had settled on the trail, for I was standing in the middle of it. Then, he stepped off and around me.

I recognized that he was not being rude, that he was simply in motion. Nonetheless, I wanted more from him. He was emerging from a region where I had never been, where I was about to spend a week, and where, because it was midwinter, I would probably meet no one else.

My questions stopped him short.

Yes, I would find water in the side canyons; there had been plenty of rain. Yes, there would be overhangs to sleep under, if I looked hard enough. His voice lacked variation in tone or pitch, as if he had forgotten these devices. Yes, I could get down to the river through some of the canyons, but if it were raining, I ought to watch out for flashfloods.

At this, his eyes clouded over. His gaze shifted. He seemed to feel he'd said too much by moving beyond the facts and into the realm of advice. Who was he to tell someone what to undertake, or not? It was, after all, a perfectly fine way to die, in the first swell of a flood. With another nod, he dismissed himself.

I came to know him better in the week that followed.

I had begun my own journey into the rain-soaked rhythms of that world. Each side canyon where I made my camp held, as he'd foretold, the perfect overhang. Some were tall enough for me to sit upright or even to stand. Most were deep enough to unfold my sleeping bag and be dry.

Just as he'd said, each shelter took some finding. Sometimes, it was upstream. Sometimes, down. Usually, it was well-hidden in the cliffs above the creek bed.

I always recognized it, for it was the one with the level bed of sand, the little rock wall windbreak, and the small, neat pile of kindling. After awhile, I knew him well enough to look until I found the kindling.

In the evenings, I huddled in my room of rock. I warmed my toes, dried my boots and socks, and quieted myself by a small, fierce fire.

I was less alone because of him. His hands had pruned the wood from the wetness. His fire had dried it. He had neatly stacked that wood with the thought of me in mind. As I had, he had sat behind the curtain of water that streamed from the rocks above, watching the cliffs drift amidst the fog.

Neither was he alone, I imagined, for the wood of his fire had been gathered, dried, and stacked by hands before his.

He had seemed so strong, so entirely self-possessed, during our one encounter, but maybe, as he'd nurtured his first fires down here, his spirit had been as fragile as mine, his capacity for solitude as tenuous. Maybe, he too had needed the thought of someone else to ride out the storm waves of self, to come into the calm.

This is how ordinary men and women withstand themselves, moving across time to join hands.

Sankar Roy

ASH COUNTRY

Red Soviet planes
     defend the sky
from the stone throwers, and far below, the blue wings
of Swallowtail butterflies
     fly to form an Afghan rug

against the charcoal canvas of a coal hill. Mothers do dishes
in a dark-skinned river, as naked kids chase a newborn calf.
A teacher draws a train with many cars
     on a blackboard
inside a rundown schoolhouse. The train's windows teem
with faces, chalk-bright in the light, as it runs
     toward a bridge,

as if following the contrail of butterflies.

Sankar Roy

A BROTHER'S ENVY

He who could bring back the rain to the roots
has spit on the clay oven
      and moved on.

Villagers say—
      This is a rock & bone place now.
No big rain will ever move this way again.
      He was the one—the only one—
who could catch the river in a conch shell.
      Peacocks, without rain,
      forget to unfold umbrella-wings
            and egrets lose their way in the heat.
The soothsayer saw him going toward the eye of a dry moon.
Without rain,
      the farmers complain.
He who could call the marble-heavy cloud is gone.
      Summer's slingshot kills the sparrows. Falling fists
      of rain don't chase the cows.
Only he could nip the candle flame with his thumb.
      Midwives deliver shadow babies, and mangoes
rot green on the branches. There is no one around
to pick up a sick dove
      and put it back into the nest.
            Everyone remembers
      the shoe-shining nights, the dance,
his playing a silver flute. Women drink thyme-water

and knit straw hats for him
all day. I match my face against his
on a photograph. My skin burns
in the influenza-nights.
  I never tell anyone of my sickness.

Hakuun Yasutani Roshi (1885-1973)

CALLIGRAPHY

Yasutani Roshi based this calligraphy on *Koan 187* "Jinteng's Rice Cake" from Master Dogen Zenji's *Shobogenzo*.

Jinteng cuts and rolls
a rice cake piece
there in the middle of the floor.

"Tell me now: one half, one whole?"
The monks just stare in *gassho*.

That fresh faced monk
with red flushed face
rises with the answer.

The translation of the calligraphy into English is by Sensei Gregory Hosho Abels and Jean Seiwa Gallagher.

The calligraphy was done in Tokyo, circa 1972.

Yasutani was a *dharma* successor of Sogaku Harada Roshi, and teacher of Koun Yamada Roshi and Taizan Maezumi Roshi.

Yasutani Calligraphy Detail
Bruce C. Kennedy

Yasutani Calligraphy Detail

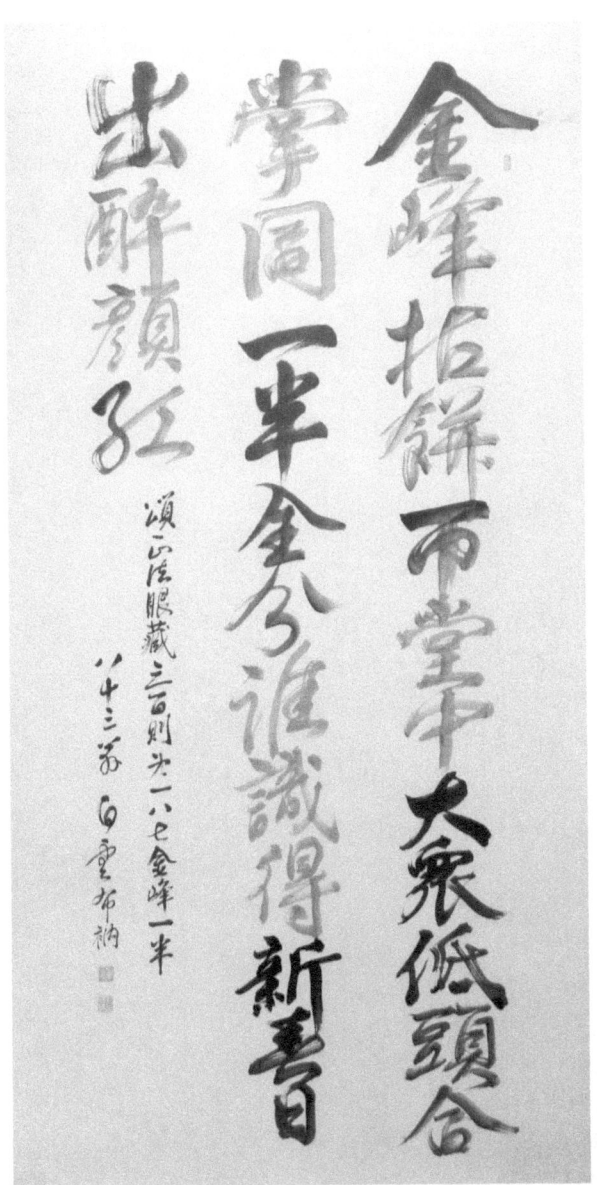

Yasutani Calligraphy

Bruce C. Kennedy

Sensei Gregory Hosho Abels

NEVER SOMETHING ELSE (EXCERPTS)

Sensei Gregory Hosho Abels began writing poetry in 1991. Inspired by *Haiku,* he expresses simple, direct experience.

He is a kind and generous teacher.

During our conversation at Still Mind Zendo in Manhattan, where he is co-resident teacher with his wife Sensei Janet Jiryu Abels, Sensei Gregory shared of his wisdom.

Pay attention.

Don't turn away from suffering.

He points out that impermanence does not mean that everything is disintegrating. It simply implies change; things fall away, even as they arise.

Sensei Gregory lives the teachings. He makes no extraneous movements. He does not elaborate. He is present with the moment.

There is the sound of hands clapping.

The following untitled poems are excerpted from *Never Something Else: Poems from the Eye of Zen,* by Sensei Gregory Hosho Abels (Seven Meadows Press, 2012).

Sensei Gregory Hosho Abels

UNTITLED POEM

if
i
could
only
understand
butterfly
faces

Sensei Gregory Hosho Abels

UNTITLED POEM

the flame's
shape
the flame's
shape
the flame's
shape

Sensei Gregory Hosho Abels

Untitled Poem

the small fish
stops short
turns in place
like a thought

Sensei Gregory Hosho Abels

UNTITLED POEM

today
the sky
is different

Sensei Gregory Hosho Abels

UNTITLED POEM

we
each
cry
in our own way

Sensei Gregory Hosho Abels

UNTITLED POEM

wet
white
waiting
paint
drying
time

Sensei Gregory Hosho Abels

UNTITLED POEM

a
frog
no
doubt
that
splash

Sensei Gregory Hosho Abels

LOOKING UP

looking up from my
homespun exhaustion
ornaments on the brown
metal brown tree thicket
why am I so emotional?
spring itself, cherry blossoms
looking like themselves, why am I so emotional?
this will not do, in the distance
ah, the distance
why am I so emotional?
do not forget what you're seeing
fumbling with images, including myself
why am I so emotional?
this will not do, not enough
tell it
tell it now, tell it to myself
tell it to myself
tell about looking up
that fumbling

Sensei Gregory Hosho Abels

TURNING BACK

walking in
to a new world
beginning to remember
that foreign feeling world
abruptly
playfully headfirst plunging in
immediately
engaged by the water
precisely daring it to trap me
coming up in one motion
quickly
turning back
without thinking
to face to see
the shore

Gayle Ellen Harvey

WHITE PEONY BLOSSOMS

What is sorrow,
with its sharps
and flats,
with its treachery,
when there are blossoms clear as
rain?

From subtlety come petals
whose force is more
deliberate
than late May in the arms
of a sober moon,
than each burning
atom,
than every clutch
of light.

Linda Swanberg

TO EARTH

You put your claim on me early.
Inside cathedrals of glaciated stone, hollow caves,
I slept long dreaming hours.

There were towering halls of painted lion and bear—
wounded healers of my soul.
The sacred recognitions I have forgotten,

yet glimpse in timeless moments.
Ancient day, I was not there when you stamped
the dark with seamless light.

My dreams birth an earlier time preserved intact,
traces of a life I cannot name, images
still etched upon my mind.

In trees, I hear dying voices of past selves—
ancestors whose lives I can only intimate,
one moment strung like galaxies across the infinite horizon.

Incomparable ground, body of earth,
in you, I find my voice. Under bold Montana skies,
I craft poems about dying trees, stars.

Mt. Sentinel and Mt. Jumbo's faces are in shambling snow.
In winter, I sweep stone paths in silence.
A pristine fawn lily braves the early spring. I watch.

Indispensable earth, where do you stop, and I begin?
We interpenetrate. I am your word—
you, my eternal question.

Jessica Young

BUTTERFLY EFFECT

We got old. Wrinkled. It's not that
we meant to. Like the crystallization
of water into snow, it happened.
We saw the way the leaves changed
each season, saw what our parents told us
we would, felt the way characters
in books felt. Not entirely bad.

flap

We got old. At times, we sought it
out. Like the slow drift of snowflakes,
it happened in a direction far from us.
When the leaves changed, we pulled
them to quicken their fall. We ached to be
parents already, to enact the written
dramas already. There was much
we saw for ourselves. All good.

flap

We got everything we wanted. At times
it was too much, like snow
when you ask for it, half a foot too much.
When the leaves changed, we were
busy looking in other directions.

When our parents died, we'd already
read books on grief. Still, there was
so much we didn't get to ask.

flap

We got more than we asked for.
When snow fell, we on the ground
were quieted, calmed.
When the leaves changed, we saved
them to remember. Their color
was dulled, but they were beautiful
for having passed through air
and time. There was so much—

Sharon Watts

BUTTERFLY

Just after the last sputter of Fourth of July fireworks has finished heralding the official mark of "high summer," I find myself vaguely sad. Nothing specific triggers this melancholy, save the observance of my denuded peony bushes, my fading roses, but the year is no longer in its blush of youth. It's showing its mortality.

And so, I shrug, find a grudging acceptance, and then embrace the deep pockets of summer that are made to hold thoughts and feelings one can only have at this time of the year.

I stand out back in the heat and sip pale green iced mint tea. I remember how my grandparents grew wild mint. Never maligned as a rampant nuisance, it was the source of summer's most perfect elixir.

To make this tea required much fresh spearmint— leaves stripped off the stalks and steeped in a pot of boiled water. The drink was then sweetened with honey straight from Pappaw's bee hives. Finally, you needed Mammaw to say, as you bounded into the house, "How about some mint tea?"

Nowadays, I make do. I have my own small patch of mint, I have my jar of local honey, and I have my filtered water. I also have the filter of memory, the memory of lazy summer afternoons spent at Mammaw and Pappaw's, days with nary a moment of melancholy yet to cloud the horizon.

Untitled Photo

Eleanor Leonne Bennett

I would spread my blanket under the black walnut tree. Time slowed to a crawl, not unlike that of the wooly bear caterpillars I encouraged to wriggle onto my cotton island in that sea of grass. I gently touched them. They would roll up into tight little balls, annoyed that I had interrupted their journeys. They were on to things more important than amusing an eleven year-old girl on a thin blanket, on a hot summer day. And yet, I was never bored.

How could I be? I had my baby blue transistor radio with me, as I sorted and spread my pack of educational butterfly flashcards all around me. How many of these exotic and mercurial beauties would I spot today? I memorized their species names as if there would be an exam at the end of the season.

"Satisfaction" played regularly on the local radio station—WFEC. I would turn it up to blast the bass. I had no idea what Mick Jagger was referring to, but I was aware of the rumblings deep in my pre-pubescent body. I hopped and danced with the uninhibited joy of a girl hip-deep in the high summer of 1964, kicking up water in a pool that felt like it would be there, forever.

My grandfather, Vernon Watts, was a self-taught Renaissance man. His job as foreman at the PP&L power plant belied the stream of his myriad interests. He could build an organ from a kit, make his own ketchup, and write poetry. He had grown up on a farm on City Island, now a recreational jewel on the Susquehanna River. It stood between Harrisburg and the suburban West Shore, where I grew up. He was no stranger to hard work or to studying the natural world around him. If his first grandchild's being born a girl was a disappointment to him, it never showed.

Or maybe he expertly played the hand he was dealt—after my father was prematurely taken out by 69,000 volts while working on a utility pole. Now, Pappaw had only me, to show and to teach, with whom he could share the things he loved, like science and nature.

During this particular summer, I received a gift from him. It was a Butterfly Preserving Kit—the next step up from my flashcards. The end result would be a perfectly preserved butterfly with a pin for display, just like you would see in a natural history museum. Anxious to follow the directions on the box, eager to please Pappaw, and excited to be on a mission of scientific discovery, I captured my first butterfly. It was one of my favorites—a *Papilio glaucas*, or Tiger Swallowtail.

Cupped in my hands, its wings beat like feather dusters against my palms. I released it into a jar that held the prerequisite cotton pad soaked with ether. I re-read the directions in the kit, and I waited.

I don't think I realized what I would actually be doing. The word "preserving" on that colorful package gave no hint that I would be killing. The butterfly struggled, and I want to say now that I opened the jar lid for it to gulp in the fresh air, for it to take off on the breeze. I even want to say just that I opened the lid, but it was too late. I didn't.

As the butterfly slowly died, I started crying. This is the freshest pain I can remember.

I was learning about nature, about a world filled with random acts of both cruelty and beauty. My education had begun in my grandparents' back yard. It would prepare me for summers beyond, summers of deep pockets, summers deep enough to hold all the butterflies in the world.

Gabriella Tal

A TORN WING

His smile was friendly, though his eyes were pleading. He sat at the round table of the restaurant-bar—a table that was too small to hold a meal, much less for someone in an electric wheelchair. His legs, supported by metal extensions, stuck out into the narrow aisle. He seemed unconcerned by the waiters, who stepped over his legs. The patrons cleared their throats uncomfortably, trying to determine how to negotiate their way across the floor. Several turned and walked the other way, for the restaurant was laid out in a circle.

"Perhaps he's used to being an obstruction," I thought, as I snuggled into my corner under the bar. I was seated in my own wheelchair. Mine was "a manual one, thank God," I thought somewhat smugly.

I was immediately embarrassed by my attitude. I had a different injury than Paul did, though I had known him for years. We'd never been close. Still, I'd met him many times— often at musical performances.

The music had not started yet, tonight. The pianist, a friend of ours, was warming up, while the guitars were tuning.

I had arrived just a moment earlier. I was exhausted. This was the end of a long day. My back often gave me trouble, when I stayed out too long. A spinal cord injury rarely hurts at the site of the injury. It hurts more in the supporting muscles below it, as they bolster up the weaker muscles. I felt pain in my tail bone, always with the sense of being "beaten." I never had been as a child.

Perhaps it was this physical aching that made me so critical of Paul.

He was, as always, with a beautiful woman. She smiled, laughing and conversing with him, while she cut his burrito into small, convenient pieces.

He was, as always, friendly to me. Still, he seemed to speak to me with an underlying resentment.

I felt uncomfortable for assuming this. Such an attitude did not fit into my own self-image. I visited the rehab center at the hospital every week to talk with patients who had recently been injured, to give them support and to suggest that we were members of the same club now. We were on the same team. I meant this sincerely.

Since my own injury fifteen years ago, I have grown in compassion. I came to believe that this compassion was, as the Buddha would have it, the most important asset of all, perhaps moreso than working knees or thighs, than being able to stand. Something good had to come of the injury, after all.

Yet, here I was with this man who was friendly and well-kept, healthy and happy looking, and I felt judgmental. I was angry that he had shown up in the same place that I had. I didn't want there to be a "wheelchair section" in the bar.

I looked over at him, and a keen strike of jealousy hit me. This man had it so easy.

My thinking was not rational. I didn't consider that his injury had left him more disabled than I was. Paul was unable even to cut his food for himself.

It was a complicated feeling, and I did not untangle it in that moment. I was jealous of his having a nice companion. I wondered cruelly how much he had to pay her to sit opposite him, smile, and be friendly. I remembered that he had a lot of money. He lived in a fancy, perfectly accessible house, with a personal chef to care for him.

But why should that aggravate me? The music began. The pick-up band found their way with each other, through loose unfitting notes that did not belong anywhere.

There was much good humor in the bar. It frustrated me that, tucked under the bar counter as I was, I could not converse with anyone.

Paul was eating his burrito.

A woman who knew me came into the bar. She had long dreadlocks. She was someone who would stand out on the street, or in an airport. Her face was pink and pure. She re-introduced herself.

I remembered her from someplace but could not recall where.

Another fellow wearing clothes that barely covered his obese frame came in. He looked unkempt. His navel stuck out of his big belly. He appeared to be in a foul mood. He climbed across Paul's legs and headed for the bar.

The man sitting on a barstool just behind me had a hearty and ready laugh. I was drawn to him, but I could not easily make a conversation from my vantage point.

I was there to listen to the music, I reminded myself. I tried to make myself comfortable with all the other lonely hearts in the bar. I was very lonely.

I listened to a few songs and interacted with no one. I was tired. I was uncomfortable with my emotions. I left suddenly.

Another musician had arrived. He was about to set his guitar amp down in a spot that would have blocked my only way out. When you are in a wheelchair, you always think about the escape hatch. *I might get trapped*, I thought, almost in a panic. *I might get caught, trapped in the bar during the set.*

With a swift, intuitive sweep across the floor, I asked him to let me out, before he got settled. He kindly acquiesced. Soon, I made it to the parking lot without a goodbye, nod, or wave to anyone.

Why I felt more pitiful than anyone else in that bar, I cannot say. I don't usually hang out in bars. Parties with lots of people are hard for me. I avoid them. I prefer small gatherings of friends, or family dinners.

Wheelchairs create a world, a new reality, a different context. And who would have understood this more than Paul? Why, then, had I separated myself from him? Why did I not want to be associated with him? Why did I not want to be seen as "like him" by others? Why did I begrudge him his wealth or his kind and attractive friend? I pondered these questions throughout the following week. I felt that there was some key in this tableau for me to understand my current situation.

* * *

A week and a half later, I was sitting by the goldfish pond behind my house, as rain gently caressed the earth. The smell of soil and the gratitude of dry trees rose like a deep-bouqueted perfume.

I have taken to breathing the air profoundly, since my accident. I cannot walk on the earth, so I anchor myself through sky.

I was no longer consciously musing on the incident at the bar.

Suddenly, it breezed through me with the sweetness of the wet wind. *He is me.*

The goldfish came to the surface of the pond, thinking the raindrops might be food. *A part of me too must be pleading,* I thought. *A part of me must be uncertain that I deserve friendship, unless I pay for it. A part of me has had to adjust to being "in the way" and, in order to live a life close to the rest of humanity, has become comfortable with taking up the extra space to do so.*

My kitten peeked out from under the ramp, keeping dry while absorbing the atmosphere of the much-needed rainfall. *Paul has adapted to his situation quite similarly to the way I have—successfully,* I thought. I hugged myself from the chill.

I noted how Paul's successful adjustment still made him stand out in the bar. The glare of self-recognition was more than I could bear.

Hating him for what I saw as his mistaken belief that he could be a part of things, I projected my own insecurities. I sat for a long time by the pond. I stared at the trees. Standing like uneven stripes in a weaving, they softened under my gaze. Frogs began to sing, and the bushes hummed with re-awakening life.

Paul, who had invited me over to his home and showed me all around. Paul, who wanted nothing more than to be seen as "whole" by everyone. Paul, who like me, didn't want to be pitied.

Seeing his open friendly face that night, a part of me had shouted inside, "But you are far from whole, you fool." Like I wanted to hurt him. I can still see his eyes, young in spirit behind his glasses, falling into shadow, as if my thoughts had reached him.

The earth began to darken in color, as the slow, steady thrum of rain fell upon it. I didn't mind that my clothes and face were becoming quite wet. A part of me was shouting at myself. Heat flushed through me. Tears and recognition braided together.

Every person in that bar had some sense of not being whole. The woman with the dreadlocks who stood out so boldly from the crowd, the large man whom I'd met a week earlier at the outdoor market, and even the cheerful man whom I liked so much. I was drawn to him, because he appeared to be whole, but scratch the surface and who knows. The musicians—I knew enough about them to remember their pain and struggles. My friend the pianist had a difficult ex-wife. Another, whom I knew through the grapevine, had an alcohol problem. Paul was as whole as anyone there.

I looked out at the protective woods surrounding me. My experience of life is more and more sheer these days. When I lean towards the transparency, there is a glint of light in the gray shadows beyond. Then, I become dizzy and am thrown back.

Aren't we all moths with a torn wing fluttering towards the light?

The grim reaper looks back over his shoulder at each of us, and do we not shake just a little?

Perhaps those who have sat as close to his scythe as Paul and I have find a chance to be a bit more whole—at least for a time—by dint of understanding something of that mystifying promise. Still, forgetfulness makes fools of us all, and the further we sit from the doorway of death, the more the material world seems real and vitally important.

It is as it should be.

But always we are broken. That is how it is to be human. And when we discover that we are whole, this world as we know it will have shattered for us, into pieces.

CONTRIBUTOR NOTES

Sensei Gregory Hosho Abels is a Zen teacher (Sensei) in the Soto White Plum Lineage of Taizan Maezumi Roshi, a *dharma* heir of Roshi Robert Jinsen Kennedy, and co-resident teacher of Still Mind Zendo in Manhattan with his wife, Sensei Janet Jiryu Abels. He has studied poetry with Jean Valentine, J. D. McClatchy, Stuart Friebert, and Debra Weinstein. For fifty years, he has enjoyed a career as an actor, stage director, and master teacher of acting. His *dharma* name, Hosho, loosely translated, means "Voice of the *Dharma*." He lives in Greenwich Village and Seven Meadows Farm in the Hudson Valley, where many of his poems are written.

Coleman Barks is a renowned poet and the bestselling author of *The Soul of Rumi* (HarperOne, 2002), *Rumi: The Book of Love* (HarperOne, 2003), and *The Essential Rumi* (HarperOne, 2004). He was prominently featured in both of Bill Moyers' PBS television series on poetry, "The Language of Life" and "Fooling with Words." He taught English and poetry at the University of Georgia for thirty years. He now focuses on writing, readings, and performances. Most recently, he has published *Rumi: The Big Red Book* (HarperOne, 2011) and *Winter Sky: Selected Poems, 1968-2008* (University of Georgia Press, 2008), a collection of his personal poetry.

Eleanor Leonne Bennett is a 15-year-old internationally acclaimed photographer and artist. Her work has been awarded by *National Geographic*, the World Photography Organisation, *Nature's Best Photography,* Papworth Trust, Mencap, The Woodland Trust, and Postal Heritage. Her photography has also been published in the *Telegraph*, the *Guardian*, BBC News website, and on the cover of books and magazines in the United states and Canada. Her art has been shown in London, Paris, Indonesia, Los Angeles, Florida, Washington, Scotland, Wales, Ireland, Canada, Spain, Germany, Japan, and Australia. Her work has been included in the Bigger Picture Global Exhibition Tour with the United Nations International Year of Biodiversity 2010 and the Environmental Photographer of the Year Exhibition 2011, among others. www.eleanorleonnebennett.zenfolio.com

Janine Canan is a California psychiatrist, award-winning author, and long-time Amma devotee. Her books include a collection of short stories *Journeys with Justine* (Regent Press, 2007); *Goddesses, Goddesses: Essays* (Regent Press, 2007); *In the Palace of Creation: Selected Works 1969-1999* (Scars Publications, 2003); and others. Janine also edited *Messages from Amma: In the Language of the Heart* (Celestial Arts, 2004) and translated *Star in My Forehead* (Holy Cow! Press, 2000), a collection of poetry by Else Lasker-Schüler.

Jessica Chen is from Taipei, Taiwan. She attended the writing program at the Savannah College of Art and Design in Savannah, Georgia and received her B.F.A. in 2011. "Probable Impossibility" is her first published story.

Noel Conneely has had work published in *Poetry Ireland*, *Chelsea, Willow Review*, *Main Street Rag*, and other publications in Ireland, England, and the United States.

Michael Dobrovolsky recently left his position in linguistics at the University of Calgary to focus on writing. His work has appeared in *Midnight Express* and *Mysterical-E*. Over the years he has worked and traveled in England, Japan, Turkey, and Russia.

Stuart Friebert is the author of *Speak Mouth to Mouth* (WordTechCommunications, 2009). This is his thirteenth book of poems. His eighth volume of translations, in co-translation with the author, is *The Swing in the Middle of Chaos: Selected Poems of Sylvia Fischerova* (Bloodaxe Books, 2010). He has also published a number of stories and memoir pieces.

Betty Gabrielli was born in 1936 and lives in Oberlin, Ohio. She was awarded an Ohio Arts Council fellowship. Her poems have appeared in a number of regional and national publications, most recently in *Ship of Fools* and *Roger*.

John Grey is an Australian-born poet who has been a U.S. resident since the late seventies. He works as a financial systems analyst. His writings have recently been published in *Connecticut Review*, *Kestrel*, and *Writer's Bloc*, with work forthcoming in *Pennsylvania English*, *Alimentum*, and the *Great American Poetry Show*.

Gayle Elen Harvey calls poetry "not art, but breathing." She is the author of seven chapbooks, the most recent being *Vanishing Points* (Sow's Ear, 2004). Her poetry has appeared in numerous literary journals, including *American Poetry Journal*, *Smartish Pace*, *Plainsong*, the *Louisiana Review*, *Willow Springs*, and *Gulf Coast*. She has been the recipient of many awards, including a New York Foundation for the Arts fellowship and the Emily Dickinson Award from the Poetry Society of America.

Vivekanand Jha is a poet and research scholar from India. He composes poems on contemporary and relevant themes. He is also completing his Ph.D. on the poetry of the noted Indian English poet Jayanta Mahapatra from Lalit Narayan Mithila University Darbhanga under the close supervision and intimate guidance of Dr. A. K. Bachan, Professor of English. Vivekanand Jha is the son of noted professor and award-winning poet Dr. Rajanand Jha, crowned with the Sahitya Akademi Award, New Delhi. His poems have been published in the following magazines: *Danse Macabre*, *Vox Poetica*, *Writing Raw*, *Tribal Soul Kitchen*, *Winamop*, *Literature India*, *Mother Bird*, *Kalinga Times*, *Holy Rose Review*, and others.

Rick Kempa lives in Rock Springs, Wyoming, where he teaches writing and philosophy at Western Wyoming College. "Into the Calm" is part of a manuscript-in-the-making based on his lifetime of hiking the Colorado Plateau. A book of his poems, *Keeping the Quiet*, was published by Bellowing Ark Press in 2008. Additional biographical and publication information can be found at wiki.wyomingauthors.org/Rick+Kempa.

Bruce Kennedy is a self-taught photographer. His eye has been informed by a lifetime of looking at paintings. It operates through unmediated listening to his body's responses to what is seen. While taking photographs, he has no particular goal in mind for them, but he does have a process goal: that of pure looking and pure response. He lives in Brooklyn and works in Manhattan, in children's publishing. His work has been exhibited at Smile Gallery in Brooklyn. His work can be viewed at http://brucekennedyphotos.zenfolio.com/.

David Lipsky is a contributing editor at *Rolling Stone* magazine. His fiction and nonfiction have appeared in the *New Yorker*, *Harper's* magazine, *The Best American Short Stories*, *The Best American Magazine Writing*, the *New York Times*, the *New York Times Book Review*, and many other publications. He contributes as an essayist to NPR's "All Things Considered," and is the recipient of a Lambert Fellowship, a Media Award from GLAAD, and a National Magazine Award. He's the author of the novel *Art Fair* (Bloomsbury Publishing, 1997), a collection of stories *Three Thousand Dollars* (Summit Books, 1989), the bestselling nonfiction book *Absolutely American* (Vintage, 2004), which was a *Time* magazine Best Book of the Year, and a nonfiction book *Of Course You End Up Becoming Yourself* (Broadway Books, 2010), about a road trip with David Foster Wallace. He is the son of painter Pat Lipsky.

Pat Lipsky has dedicated herself to painting for several decades. She graduated from Cornell University with a B.F.A. in 1963. She then attended the graduate program in painting at Hunter College, where she studied with sculptor Tony Smith, and received an M.A. in 1968. Ms. Lipsky's paintings have been reviewed by Ken Johnson (*The New York Times*), David Cohen (*The New York Sun*), Alicia Turner (*The Miami Herald*), Karen Wilkin (*Art in America*), and Alexi Worth (*The New Yorker*), among others. Her paintings are in twenty-one museum collections, including the Whitney, the Hirshhorn, and the San Francisco Museum of Modern Art. She has had twenty-eight solo exhibitions. Her work is currently handled by DC Moore Gallery in New York.

Jayanta Mahapatra has authored eighteen books of poems. The publication of his first book of poems, *Svayamvara and Other Poems* (A Writers Workshop Publication, 1971) was followed by the publication of *Close the Sky, Ten By Ten* (Dialogue Publications, 1971). His collections of poems include *A Rain of Rites* (University of Georgia Press, 1976), *Life Signs* (Oxford University Press, 1984), and *A Whiteness of Bone* (Viking, 1992). One of Mahapatra's better remembered works is the long poem "Relationship," for which he won the Sahitya Akademi award in 1981. He is the first Indian English Poet to receive the honor. Besides being one of the most popular Indian poets of his generation, Mahapatra was also part of the trio of poets who laid the foundations of modern Indian English Poetry. He shared a special bond with A. K. Ramanujan.

Eric Mothes was raised in Houston, Texas by a single mother, Jennifer Mothes. He lives and writes to inspire the un-inspirable. His life is an example of second chances and God's mercy. His words represent struggles that will inevitably lead to success. In May of 2010, he finished his first chapbook,

Pretty Boy Swag. He currently attends Concordia University in Austin, Texas.

Simon Perchik is an attorney whose poems have appeared in *Partisan Review*, the *New Yorker*, *Lalitamba*, and elsewhere. For more information, including his essay "Magic, Illusion, and Other Realities," and for a complete bibliography, please visit his website at www.simonperchik.com.

Ines P. Rivera Prosdocimi completed her M.F.A. in Creative Writing at American University in May of 2009. Her work has appeared or is forthcoming in the *Afro-Hispanic Review*, *Alaska Quarterly Review*, *Bellevue Literary Review*, *Borderlands*: *Texas Poetry Review*, *Border Senses*, *Brush Mountain Review*, *Callaloo*, *Hispanic Cultural Review*, *PALABRA*, *Pterodáctilo*, *Poet Lore*, *Revista LENGUA*, *Saranac Review*, and the *Caribbean Writer*.

Patrice C. Queen is a poet, writer, exhibit curator, and public speaker. She uses the arts to facilitate the shift needed to create healing from all forms of violence and oppression. She addresses social justice issues through Forum Theater. www.dwafanm.org

Drew Roberts is currently living in upstate New York and working on his first novel.

Sankar Roy, originally from India, is a poet, translator, activist, and multimedia artist, who lives near Pittsburgh, Pennsylvania. He is the author of three chapbooks. His poems have appeared in more than eighty journals and anthologies. His first full-length book is *Moon Country* (Tebot Bach, 2009).

Jalal ad-Din Muhammad Rumi (1207-1273) was a Persian poet and Sufi mystic. He was deeply inspired by the love he felt for his teacher and companion Shams-e Tabrizi.

Denise Shekerjian is the author of *Uncommon Genius* (Viking, 1990; Penguin, 1991, 2001). Her short stories and essays have appeared in the *Baltimore Review*, the *Chariton Review*, the *Massachusetts Review*, *North Dakota Quarterly*, and others. She is the recipient of two Pushcart Prize nominations, a Graybar American History Prize, and a Marshall Fellowship in Civil Liberties.

Fred Sievert retired in 2007 as the President of the New York Life Insurance Company, a Fortune 100 company. In May of 2011 he received his M.A. in Religion from Yale Divinity School. He serves on several for-profit and not-for-profit boards, while teaching at the Dolan Business School of Fairfield University, and mentoring four young corporate executives. Mr. Sievert is currently writing a book and has published essays recounting many of his inspirational business and personal experiences. These have appeared in *A Gathering of Tribes* and *Ken*Again*.

Jyotsna Sreenivasan grew up in northeastern Ohio, though her parents are immigrants from India. Her stories have appeared in numerous literary magazines and anthologies. Her first novel is *And Laughter Fell From the Sky* (HarperCollins, 2012). She currently lives in northern Idaho with her husband and sons.

Linda Swanberg of Missoula, Montana, received her M.A. from the University of Montana in the 1970s. Since 2003, she has studied with Tobin Simon, Director of the Proprioceptive Writing Center. Her work has appeared in the *South Carolina Review*, the *Cape Rock*, *Carquinez Poetry Review*, *Owen Wister Review*, the *Meridian Anthology of Contemporary Poetry*, *CQ (California Quarterly)*, and *HeartLodge*, among others. Her writings are forthcoming in *North Atlantic Review*, the *Griffin*, and *Quiddity International Literary Journal*. Swanberg lives with her husband, Gregg, and collie, Chanel, She is a musician. She also tends a woodland garden, which has been her main focus for the last twenty-seven years.

Gabriella Tal has been a lover of Meher Baba (knowingly) for twenty years. She lives in Chapel Hill, North Carolina and makes numerous trips to her Beloved's home in Ahmednagar, India. A therapist and musician, she has written music to many of Bhau Kalchuri's *ghazals*. Her greatest joy is to sing for him. Her CD *Happiness is Better* (2004), produced at Bhau's direction, contains twenty of his *ghazals* sung by herself and other Baba lovers.

Sharon Watts is an accomplished illustrator and visual artist. She has archived a collection of stories to commemorate a 9/11 F.D.N.Y. hero, *Miss You, Pat: Collected Memories of N.Y.'s*

Bravest of the Brave, Captain Patrick J. Brown (Lulu, 2007). This is her first book. She has also finished a collection of journal essays entitled *Coming To My Senses* and is working on a memoir of her art student days in N.Y.C., in the early 1970s.

Alexander Weinstein is the Director of the Martha's Vineyard Institute of Creative Writing. He has worked as a creative writing teacher and freelance editor for the past ten years. He leads fiction workshops in the United States and Europe, and teaches at Siena Heights University. His fiction has appeared in *Pleiades*, *Sou'Wester*, *Notre Dame Review*, the *Rio Grande Review*, *Hawai'i-Pacific Review*, the *MacGuffin*, and other journals.

Hakuun Yasutani (1885-1973) was a Soto Roshi and the founder of the Sanbo Kyodan Zen Buddhist organization.

Jessica Young currently holds a Zell Fellowship for poetry in Ann Arbor, Michigan. She completed her M.F.A. at the University of Michigan and her undergraduate work at M.I.T. Her poetry has been nominated for a Pushcart Prize and has appeared most recently in *Bellingham Review*, *Copper Nickel*, and *Versal*.

bluestem

45130

SUPPORT REFUGE

P.O. Box; 131 Planetarium Station; New York, NY 10024

Lalitamba is in partnership with Refuge, a holistic shelter in New York City. Through years of working with people in need of permanent housing, we understand how stressful the situation can be. Refuge offers all the comforts of home to women in transition. *To make a tax-deductible donation to Refuge, please send a check to Lalitamba-Refuge at the above address.* Your generosity makes it all possible. Thank you!

www.threejewelsrefuge.org

SUBSCRIBE

P.O. Box; 131 Planetarium Station; New York, NY 10024

_____$10 One-year subscribtion (one issue)

_____$19 Two-year subscription (two issues)

Please add $4.95 for postage and handling and enclose a check written to *Lalitamba*.

Begin my subscription with issue number _____

Name_____

Address_____

City, State, Zip_____

Please send a gift subscription to:

Begin the subscription with issue number _____

Name_____

Address_____

City, State, Zip_____

www.ingramcontent.com/pod-product-compliance
Lightning Source LLC
Chambersburg PA
CBHW031330170626
46807CB00002B/625